Heading *for* Home

To Jim —

Hope you enjoy the book.

Best wishes,

Ken Tucson

Heading *for* Home

Kent Stock

with

Ken Fuson

Heading For Home: My Journey from Little League to Hollywood

Interior Design: Chad Kreel

Cover Photo: Kliks Photography

Heading For Home, ISBN: 978-1-886296-54-1

Co-Published by:
Arrow Publications, Inc.
P.O. Box 10102
Cedar Rapids, IA 52410

Telephone: (319) 395-7833
Toll Free: (877) 363-6889 (U.S. Only)
www.arrowbookstore.com

Printed in the United States of America, July 2009

I dedicate this book to Coach Jim Van Scoyoc, who taught me more than just baseball, and to everyone who has ever worn a Norway baseball jersey.

Contents

Introduction

What would I tell them?

I paced the third-base coaching box. We trailed 4-3, in the top of the seventh and final inning of the Class 1A Iowa high school baseball championship game. There were two outs, nobody on base. Our first baseman, Kyle Schmidt, had two strikes on him. We were one pitch away from losing.

Poor Kyle. He was a great kid, a gentle bear of a young man, but he was really struggling at the plate that summer. He had already struck out twice in this game. A senior, he had, over the years, come to the plate 13 times in state championship play. He had never gotten a hit.

I wasn't giving up – not on this team – but it's a coach's job to stay three steps ahead, to prepare for any eventuality. On this sunny afternoon of August 3, 1991, in Marshalltown, few people would have bet on a rally. The odds were overwhelming that I soon would be addressing the losing team in the championship game. Perhaps if I had 30 years of coaching experience to draw upon, the words would flow easily. *Great season, guys. Keep your heads up. Second place is a worthy accomplishment.*

But this was the Norway, Iowa, baseball team. Boys there didn't play for second place.

I first learned of the Norway tradition when I was a youngster, growing up in Ankeny, just north of Des Moines. Somehow, this tiny town of Norway – the population was 586 – captured one state baseball title after another. During the regular season, Norway routinely played the largest schools in the state – from Cedar Rapids, Waterloo and Iowa City, for example – and beat them.

The town produced two legendary coaches, Bernie Hutchison and Jim Van Scoyoc, and several professional baseball players, including Hal Trosky, a hitting star for Cleveland and the Chicago White Sox in the 1930s and '40s; Mike Boddicker, who won a World Series title with Baltimore in 1983, the highlight of a 14-season major-league career; and Bruce Kimm, who was the personal catcher for Detroit's Mark "The Bird" Fidrych in the mid-1970s and the manager of the Chicago Cubs for a few months in 2002.

It was an absolute long shot that I ended up as Norway's head baseball coach in that spring and summer of 1991. I was the varsity girls' volleyball coach in Belle Plaine, another small town about 20 miles from Norway. A chance meeting with Van Scoyoc led to my serving as his assistant during the 1990 baseball season. That year, Norway won the Class 1A baseball title, the school's 19th state championship. It was one of the greatest summers of my life.

But Norway was facing some of the same economic pressures squeezing many other small towns. The state wanted smaller schools to consolidate, to share programs, in the belief that students would benefit from a broader array of courses and opportunities. People in town protested. Lose the high school, they said, and we'll lose our identity.

This was one competition Norway couldn't win. The state was too powerful, and the decision was made: Norway would merge with nearby Benton Community High School of Van Horne at the start of the 1991-92 school year.

Van Scoyoc (pronounced skoy, rhymes with boy) hated the decision, and wasn't shy about who knew it. When he wasn't offered a teaching contract at Benton, he left Norway to be the pitching coach for one of the Detroit Tigers' farm teams.

So that's how, in the summer of 1991, I ended up replacing the Tony LaRussa of Iowa high school baseball coaches. I was 29 years old, and was given a one-year contract. After one final season, Norway High School, its baseball team and my coaching future there would cease to exist.

I knew how high the stakes were, but if I didn't, the players quickly reminded me. At one of our first team meetings, I asked them to set their goals for the upcoming season. One of the seniors raised his hand.

"Coach, we only have one goal: to win Norway's 20th state title in our last season."

And now, on a hot summer afternoon in Marshalltown, where the state held its baseball tournaments, we were one strike away from falling agonizingly short.

"Come on, Kyle," I said, clapping my hands. "Get something started."

I paced the third-base box, thinking about the dejected faces I was about to confront on that field. How could I possibly comfort them? I was still grasping for the right words when the opposing pitcher fired the ball.

What happened next would inspire a movie to be written, filmed and shown in theaters throughout the country. Sean Astin, who portrayed Rudy in the great football movie of the same name, as well as Samwise Gamgee in the "Lord of the Rings" trilogy, would add a new character to his repertoire: me.

That game set in motion one of the most exhilarating roller-coaster rides of my life, with pinch-me highs and tear-soaked lows. That season, and that game, changed my life.

Looking back, the idea that a girls' volleyball coach would lead a storied high school baseball team in its final season would most likely strike any rational person as one of the greatest flukes in coaching history. I was, as they say, in the right place at the right time.

But it was a place and a time that I had been preparing for my entire life, and it's a journey, I hope, that might give others the courage to chart their own paths, because I learned a valuable lesson that summer:

Anything's possible.

1
Leading Off

I was going to be a baseball player.

My classmates might have changed their career aspirations over the years, shifting from cowboy to astronaut to rock star, but when the elementary teachers asked me, I was reliably consistent.

I was going to play professional baseball, preferably for the St. Louis Cardinals, my favorite team, and preferably with Bob Gibson, my favorite player. Which would have been a decent trick, given that he was a grown man in his pitching prime and I was a second-grader in Ankeny. But dreams rarely cede ground to common sense.

My mother, Janet, tried to warn me that I needed a backup plan. As she puts it now, "I tried to tell him there are a lot of kids who think they're going to be baseball players."

She knew reality has a nasty way of interfering with a person's dreams. She had heard stories growing up on an Iowa farm of how her father – my grandfather – wanted nothing more than to graduate from college, but life threw him a curveball and he ended up on a tractor.

To me, though, Mom's advice demonstrated a disappointing lack of faith in my future prospects. Question my ability, will ya? You watch, Mom,

I said. When I make the majors, I'll just send Dad a ticket. You'll have to buy your own.

The truth is, my parents have always been my biggest fans. They never pushed me to play sports, but they encouraged the interest that was always there.

I'll give you two examples, one for each parent.

When I was in third or fourth grade, my mom pulled my younger brother, Lee, and me out of class because Brooks Robinson was signing autographs for a promotion at an Ankeny sporting goods store.

I'm not sure which surprised me more – that my mother would allow us to skip class, or that I'd have a chance to meet Brooks Robinson, the Hall of Fame third baseman for the Baltimore Orioles. It was just the coolest thing ever. I've never forgotten it.

Several years later, in August 1971, my dad, Ken, was reading in the morning newspaper that Gibson would be going after his 200th victory that night. Dad woke us up and said he was driving the family six hours to St. Louis to see it. I was 9 years old. It was the first of many trips to watch the Cardinals.

When we arrived, we learned that Gibson had been scratched and Jerry Reuss would be taking his place. We watched Reuss and the Cardinals lose, 6-1, to the San Diego Padres, and then spent the night in a Howard Johnson parking lot, all five of us -- my parents, my brother, sister, and me -- crammed into the family Volkswagen. The next night, we returned to Busch Stadium, and I watched my idol Gibson beat the San Francisco Giants, 7-2. Again, an unforgettable memory, just as my parents must have figured it would be.

•

Mom claims she was my first coach. I'll take her word for it, because I was too young to remember.

She recalls playing catch with me, which involved her tossing a ball into the playpen and my picking it up and firing it back to her. She says my eye-hand coordination was remarkable, but what would you expect a proud mom to say?

I couldn't wait to join the older kids. We had bases set up all over the house. Mom says I always slid into home plate, just as I'd seen the real players do. When I was old enough to play outside, my friends and I spent so much time in the backyard that my parents figured grass would never again grow there.

A lifelong love affair had begun. Baseball is the thread that connects the various strands of my life. I don't question how or why it started, because it was always there.

"We all just knew that baseball was his life," my dad says.

I love everything about the game. I love the smell of a freshly mowed outfield, the precision of the chalk lines leading to first base, the balletic grace of a perfectly turned 6-4-3 double play. I love that sharp *pop!* of a fastball slamming into a catcher's mitt, the "beer here" cry of a vendor at the ballpark, the thunderous sound heard in my backyard when one of us sent a ball crashing onto the metal roof of the farm implement shed south of our house.

I agree with the late Jack Buck, the great Cardinals' radio announcer, with whom I shared many a summer evening. He once said the wonderful thing about going to a baseball game was the chance that you might see something you had never seen before. An unassisted triple play. Four home runs, back to back to back to back. A perfect game. You never know.

More than anything, I loved the countless individual decisions, from player and manager alike, that often determined which team won. Do I throw home, attempting to get the tying run, or to second base, keeping the go-ahead run at first? Do I keep my tiring pitcher in for one more hitter? Do I try to sneak a fastball past a dead-pull hitter?

All sports appealed to me, and I participated in most, but baseball fascinated me. I don't know whether my coaches ever noticed it, but I listened to them, really listened, and tried to soak up every piece of information they offered. I wanted to know everything there was to know about the sport. I played basketball, but I studied the strategy of baseball. There's a difference.

School? I did fine, and earned decent grades, but I never worked at it. I was going to be a baseball player, not an academic. At a parent-teacher conference, one of the teachers told my parents that it might be a nice change of pace if Kent wrote a book report on something other than a baseball player.

What I studied then were the sports pages of The Des Moines Register. Back then, its sports pages were printed on peach-colored paper, and the section was called The Big Peach. I checked the box scores as carefully as Bible scholars search for clues. It was in those pages that I first heard of a small town called Norway, Iowa, which seemed to win a state baseball title every year. I urged my parents to move to what sounded to me like a baseball paradise. They declined, but I got there eventually.

Once each year, on a Sunday, the Register published the list of the all-state baseball players, printing each player's photograph, name and school, like a junior version of the Hall of Fame. I studied those faces and the names of the schools. Someday, I vowed to myself, I would earn one of those coveted spots. It may have been nothing more than a boy's fantasy, but it felt as real to me as the notion that I would be playing pro baseball one day. I couldn't imagine doing anything else.

•

Baseball, and Bob Gibson, also figured prominently in my summer vacations.

Each summer, I'd spend a week with my cousin, Todd Johnson, in Omaha. As any careful reader of Gibson's biography, "From Ghetto to Glory," knows, he grew up in Omaha and lived there with his family in the off-season. I had read the book so often, I nearly had it memorized.

As it happened, Todd's home was close enough to the Gibson residence that their families shared a neighborhood swimming pool. I remember riding our bicycles past Gibson's home, hoping to catch a glimpse of my hero, but he was in the middle of the baseball season. We did see his wife and daughters in their driveway, which was exciting. We left them alone, which was probably exciting for them.

Of course, it's common for boys to hold baseball players as heroes, but there was something different about Gibson. He was the person who introduced me to the country's civil rights struggle. Ankeny was about as lily-white a community as you could have found in the late 1960s. We had a young black person stay at our house for a week when I was a boy, but that's about as much contact as I had with someone who wasn't white. I still remember some of the stares we attracted as we rode our bicycles around town.

So when I saw, from the safety of my living room, televised scenes of white Southern sheriffs setting dogs and turning hoses on blacks, it wasn't difficult for me to imagine them doing the same to Gibson. I empathized with him, and with them. I knew whose side I was on.

We have many mentors in life, and I often advise young people to seek them out. Although I have never met him, Gibson was one of mine. His book was my first introduction to racism. His performance on the pitcher's mound was my first glimpse of sustained athletic excellence. His life was a portrait in dignity.

But the first and most important mentor in my life was my father.

I don't remember a day he was absent. If the weather was decent, we played catch every night, no matter how tired he was from a day of teaching. Sometimes Gene Scheffers, a family friend, arrived to keep us company. We played catch so often that Dad finally bought a catcher's mitt. I had worn out his regular glove. Those memories remain vivid.

My dad and I are best friends now, but I feared him when I was younger. Not because of anything he had done or might do – I don't remember a single spanking – but because I was afraid of letting him down. I never wanted to get that stern look that suggested I had disappointed him. He commanded respect without yelling.

One time, in Little League, I apparently caused quite a scene. I was a hot-tempered kid who hated to lose. I still hate it, whether on the golf course or in a bowling alley. After striking out, I must have thrown my helmet or bat, because the next thing I knew, Dad had pulled me aside.

"Don't you ever do that again," he warned me. "Don't embarrass yourself or your family."

He didn't have to tell me twice.

Everything I have ever accomplished, I owe to my parents. So before we go much further, I should probably tell you how they met, and how a side trip to St. Louis to see the Cardinals play became part of their honeymoon itinerary.

I told you I was born to love baseball.

2
My First Team

Thank goodness Don Brooks had more courage than my dad did. Otherwise, I might not be here.

The date was October 27, 1956. A cousin of Mom's, Ramona Egemo, was marrying a friend of Dad's, Lee Arrowsmith, at Immanuel Lutheran Church in Story City, Iowa. Dad was an usher. And one of the young women he found himself escorting down the aisle was my mother, Janet Lee, an elementary school teacher in Hubbard who had grown up on a 160-acre farm near McCallsburg.

"It was obviously love at first sight," my dad says now.

But he wasn't about to tell Mom that. Not my dad. He was a preacher's son, and he accepted his own mother's notion that the children of pastors should be seen and not heard. Of the two, my mom is the social butterfly, my dad more reticent.

So reticent, in fact, that after the ceremony, at the reception in the church basement, he couldn't work up the nerve to introduce himself to Mom. Instead, he stared at her, and continued staring at her.

My Uncle Chuck noticed. He was 7.

"Janet, that guy over there is staring at you," he told my mom. She ignored him.

A little bit later, Chuck repeated his observation.

"OK," Mom said, "if I looked now, will he be looking?"

"Sure."

Mom looked up. Sure enough, Ken Stock was looking right at her.

On Dad's side of the room, Don Brooks noticed how smitten his friend was, and he urged Dad to introduce himself. But Dad couldn't do it. Too nervous. So it was Don who walked over to my mother and said, "Can I introduce you to Kenny Stock?"

And that's how my parents met.

Dad apparently located his backbone, because he asked whether he could escort Mom home. Now it was her turn to get nervous. This was 1956, after all. Drive a girl home? He might as well have asked for a smooch.

"I'd never gone home with anybody I didn't know," she said.

So she approached her father, Franklin Lee.

"Dad, I don't know what to do," she remembers saying. "This Kenny Stock – I don't know anything about him – asked me if he could take me home."

Grandpa Lee, as usual, offered sage advice. "Ramona knows him," he said. "Ask her for a recommendation."

Ramona was changing out of her wedding dress when Mom knocked on the door.

"There's a Kenny Stock who's asked to take me home, and Dad says I should ask you if I should go."

"Oh, you can't go wrong," Ramona said.

And that's how my parents went on their first date.

•

Dad most likely filled in some of his biographical blanks on that drive home and in the following weeks.

He was born in Cherokee, Iowa, and lived there for five years. The family – Dad was one of five children – then moved to Ayrshire, and Dad remained there from kindergarten through October of his junior year. The family moved again, this time to Coon Rapids, where Dad completed his senior year and graduated in 1954.

Dad loved sports – I must have inherited that quality – and played basketball and baseball. He was a point guard in basketball and usually guarded the other team's best player. In baseball, he played second base and shortstop in Ayrshire, and then switched to catcher in Coon Rapids. "A decent hitter," he describes himself.

Dad's father – my Grandpa Stock – was a Lutheran pastor. His name was William, and he was quite talented musically. They say he could play almost any song on almost any instrument. If he heard it, he could play it.

He loved young people. He was the director of recreation at a church camp in Okoboji, in northwest Iowa, every summer for 25 years. He wrote plays in which teenagers performed. He was the master of ceremonies at social gatherings. About the only thing that slowed him down was his eyesight. He was legally blind for many years. My father used to drive him from Ayrshire so he could preach at a smaller church in nearby Webb. I remember Grandpa needing an enormous magnifying glass to read the Bible.

He was, like my father, a man whose faith never wavered. Grandpa Stock always said that when it was his turn to go to heaven, he wanted to die on Easter Sunday. He got his wish, in 1977.

One of my fondest memories is sitting with Grandpa Stock and listening to radio broadcasts of Minnesota Twins games, with Herb Carneal and Halsey Hall describing the action. I always considered the Twins my American League team – out of respect for Grandpa Stock – but I followed Dad's path and became a devout St. Louis Cardinals fan.

When Dad was a boy, there were no teams west of the Cardinals. Their radio broadcasts – with Harry Caray in his prime – blanketed the Midwest, and Dad idolized Stan Musial the way I would later look up to Bob Gibson.

Grandmother Stock – her name was Lillian – had a wry sense of humor, but also a strict sense of how a pastor's wife and family should behave. She was always last in the food line at any potluck dinner. She wanted to remain in the background.

One thing I learned later about my grandfather that I admire is that he always paid my grandmother a small stipend, telling her that she should spend the money on herself, not on the family. He may have been the pastor, but theirs was a partnership in faith. It reminds me of my own parents' relationship.

After Dad graduated from high school, he left Coon Rapids and headed to Des Moines, where he enrolled in a two-year program at the American Institute of Business. But he quit after nine months.

"I got tired of living on $15 a week," Dad says.

He and a friend rented a room from an elderly couple for $5 a week. Dad was working at an optical shop after classes, but he decided it wasn't enough, not even with the extra money my Grandma Stock would slip to him from time to time. School would have to wait. Dad needed a full-time job.

He landed at the Firestone tire plant in north Des Moines, where he made $200 a month. "I was really living," he jokes. It was enough that he could eventually buy a new, 1956 car.

Two months later, he proposed. Dad probably either figured he had met the love of his life, or he never again was going to find the courage to approach another young woman.

"I needed a cook," he says now. "I was tired of eating tomato soup."

But Mom wasn't ready.

"I liked him," she says. "But marriage was another thing."

●

Grandpa Lee had a rule: His three daughters would not work on the family farm. That included his wife, my Grandma Selma, too. The women could gather eggs and detassel corn, but the heaviest, dirtiest, smelliest work was the province of Grandpa, his three sons and the hired man.

The Lees grew corn and beans on their 160-acre farm and another one they rented. They raised livestock, chicken and pigs. It was the quintessential Iowa family farm near McCallsburg, a small town north of Ames.

My uncles have told me that Grandpa Lee could be a stern taskmaster, and I have seen his anger flare when something on the farm went wrong, like a cow that declined to move as quickly as he wanted it to. But that was a side I rarely experienced. Grandpa Lee and I had a strong bond.

Almost every summer, my cousin Todd and I would spend a week at Grandpa and Grandma Lee's, and they basically gave us our run of the place. For someone who grew up in town, where almost every neighbor within six blocks was ready to report you if you rode your bicycle on the wrong side of the street, it was a liberating adventure to explore farm life.

My mother is a woman of great and deep faith, but she also is a worrier, which made her overprotective. Grandpa and Grandma Lee weren't, and Todd and I took full advantage of it. I remember crawling in the corners of the corn crib. My mother would have fainted had she known. She might pass out now just reading about it.

What bonded Grandpa Lee and me was the same thing that connected me with so many adult men in my life – sports. He loved baseball almost as much as I did, and had somehow become a Brooklyn Dodgers fan out in the middle of Iowa.

Grandpa had been a catcher when he was younger and had banged up a thumb while playing. He had a catcher's mitt at the farm that I fell in love with. I used to walk around with it, hoping he'd eventually tell me to just keep it. But he never did, and I still wonder what happened to it.

Mom tells me that there was usually some sort of baseball or softball game occurring at the farm every night, with Grandma Lee serving as the pitcher for both teams. (My Grandma Stock used to do the same thing.)

Other than my parents, I never had bigger fans than my Grandpa and Grandma Lee. I used to call them with reports after Little League games. Later, when I played in college, they would come to the games, then call home and tell my mom and dad how I had done.

●

But if there was one thing that Grandpa Lee loved more than sports, it was the pursuit of knowledge. From the time my mother and her brothers and sisters could walk, he told them they were going to college, and all six of them did. Mom graduated from Waldorf College, in Forest City, Iowa, then Drake University, in Des Moines, Iowa, with a teaching degree.

Grandpa Lee's own story was heartbreaking. He was the oldest in a family of 8, and he was expected to stay home and help with the farm. But he went against his family's wishes and enrolled at Luther College in Decorah, Iowa.

He supported himself by working in a Decorah hotel, but was injured when somebody bumped into him, scalding him with hot coffee. He then divided his time between Luther and home, where he taught to raise money.

He eventually met his future wife, and they began raising a family, but he always planned to return and finish his work at Luther.

Back then, the college had a huge barn, and if you wanted to bring your farm animals, you could do the chores and collect the money for milk and cream. That's how many students paid their way through college, and my Grandpa Lee planned to do the same.

He wrote the college a letter, saying he was bringing his wife, three children and a truckload of animals with him. The college notified him that it had discontinued the program. He was crushed. He never did finish college, and always regretted it. He continued farming, which he never enjoyed, until he turned 50, when he became a banker.

"It's a very sad story," my mother says.

I always wondered what my Grandpa Lee might have accomplished in his life had he been able to pursue his dream. He never complained about his fate, at least within my earshot. But once Mom told me the story, I never questioned why he was so adamant that I must attend college someday. It wasn't an option, in his view.

●

After their first date, Dad drove to Hubbard, where Mom taught school, every Wednesday night. Then they would travel to a restaurant in the town of Eldora.

"I was so shy that we had to get a back booth so my back was to the people," Dad says. "I didn't want them to see me eat."

Mom confirms this.

"That was just pathetic," she says, laughing. "But that's exactly the way he was."

Dad returned on weekends, staying in the Lee house and helping out on the farm. He was used to it. One summer in high school, he lived with a farm family for three months, earning money by doing chores.

By March 9, 1957, five months after they had met, Mom finally relented and accepted Dad's engagement ring. They were married on July 27, 1957. They went to California for their honeymoon. On the way home, Dad talked Mom into making a spontaneous side trip to St. Louis to watch the Cardinals play.

"I figured it was on the way," he says.

They moved into a basement apartment in Urbandale, a Des Moines suburb. Dad continued working at Firestone; Mom taught second grade in Urbandale. She eventually quit teaching when she had my sister, Debbie, who was born on July 22, 1958. My parents brought her home on their first anniversary.

A doctor urged my parents to move out of the basement apartment, so they bought our house in Ankeny. Three years later, it was time for me to join them.

3
Safe at Home

I come from an unbroken home.

We've all read enough sports biographies to know that this is the point at which I'm supposed to introduce my lifelong addiction to alcohol, drugs or steroids. Or perhaps discuss the way my father would grab his belt if I made a crucial error in a baseball game. Or maybe this is the chapter in which I reveal how I was handed envelopes stuffed with cash if only I attended a booster's favorite college.

I almost feel as if I'm supposed to apologize, but none of that happened to me. I had a wonderful childhood. I was raised by two parents who loved their children. I was coached by men who had my best interests at heart.

Look, I know this sounds like something straight out of "Leave It to Beaver" or "Father Knows Best," and I also know that this would be a more dramatic narrative if I had some horrible dark secret to reveal. But the truth is, life was pretty swell in my Iowa neighborhood, and I was a good kid.

OK, I confess: I sometimes rode my bicycle in the street when I knew my mother told us we couldn't. Sorry, Mom, but you raised a rebel.

In fact, if I may carry this theme of a charmed life a little further, allow me to point out that the stork didn't bring me into the world. Santa Claus did.

Debbie was 2½ and desperate for a younger brother or sister. Mom says she begged for a sibling. So it probably should have surprised no one that when it was her turn to sit on Santa's lap at Merle Hay Mall in Des Moines, she had a special request.

"Would you give me a real baby?"

If he was surprised, Santa betrayed no evidence of it. Instead, he turned to my mom and dad and said, "Did you hear that?"

I was born on September 27, 1961, and Debbie has treated me like a Christmas gift ever since. My parents remember how she would entertain me for hours, trying to make me laugh. "I didn't have to do a thing," Mom says. "She handled everything."

I can't remember ever fighting or arguing with Debbie. Years later, when she was a senior in college and I was a freshman, she would send me money. I'm sure she was struggling for spending money herself, yet she'd still send me a twenty. That's the type of person she is, and that's the kind of home I was born into.

•

In those days, female teachers who got pregnant were expected to leave their jobs and raise their children, which is exactly what Mom did.

To supplement the family income, she opened what she believes was the first preschool in Ankeny. I couldn't grow up fast enough. I wanted to be doing what the older kids were doing, and by the time I was 3, I was sitting right next to them, trying to follow the lessons, and trying to keep up when they played games.

And here's the thing: I did keep up with them. For a long time, probably into high school, I could hold my own athletically with boys two and three years older. I'm not sure I was that gifted, but I was that obsessed with getting better.

After school, I'd run home and play catch with Dad until Mom called us in for supper. Then we'd go back outside. If my parents would have let me, I would have gladly given up sleep for an all-night session of catch in the backyard.

When I was one, my dad made the decision to quit working at Firestone, where he was working the dreaded 11 p.m.-to-7 a.m. shift. He knew he would have to find another occupation if he was going to coach Little League and be the kind of parent he wanted to be. So he started taking classes, first at what was then Grand View College, then at Drake University, both in Des Moines. He had decided to become a teacher.

I've always thought that was a tremendously gutsy thing for him to do, and I admire him greatly for it. He decided he wanted a better life, and he worked for it, taking classes at the same time he was working various odd jobs.

Dad started teaching at Weeks Junior High School in Des Moines in 1966 and was there 17 years, followed by another 14 years teaching applied economics at East High School, also in Des Moines. So he was leaving work about the same time Debbie and I arrived home from school. Our brother, Lee, who was born in 1964, was home with Mom, waiting for us.

•

The idea that Mom would open a preschool and Dad would become a teacher were leaps of faith, but they were never scared to jump. My parents have always lived their faith.

This is how Mom describes their marriage: "It was an answer to a prayer. He was praying the same kind of thing. He wanted a Christian woman, and

I wanted a Christian man. Church was important to both of us, and it still is. I think we felt that the Lord had brought us together."

They have been married 51 years, and both will be deeply disappointed if they don't get to spend another half-century together.

I was always involved in church, and most summers attended Riverside Lutheran Bible Camp in Story City. In sixth grade, I got my first kiss on the walking path. I can't remember her name. (I'm sure she has mine memorized. Right.)

My faith is not as public or as unquestioning as that of my parents. Those questions began in, of all places, my own grandfather's church.

Both of my parents belong to the Lutheran church, but Dad was a member of the Missouri Synod branch, while Mom was member of a different branch, the American Lutheran Church (today it's the Evangelical Lutheran Church in America). When they were married, Dad joined Mom's branch.

As I said previously, my Grandpa Stock was a Lutheran minister. He was affiliated with the Missouri Synod, and there were dozens of times when the Stocks would gather for some sort of family reunion and we'd go to Grandpa Stock's church. But we couldn't take Communion because we were in the different branch, while our relatives could because they remained in the Missouri Synod. It felt as if we were outcasts.

It was the same reason my grandfather was not allowed to officiate at my parents' wedding, I learned later.

It bothered me. I wasn't scarred for life, but it gnawed at me. When I was older, I asked a Missouri Synod pastor to explain it to me. He tried, but I never accepted the notion that my own grandfather couldn't give me Communion.

•

I didn't ask Santa Claus for a little brother, which probably explains why Lee and I had a relationship more typical of rival siblings. (I didn't send him any money in college, either.) We're great friends today, but I can remember many basketball games in the driveway in which I responded to a good play from him or one of his little friends by knocking them down.

Here's a great Lee story:

When we were little, my parents, being the teachers they were, decided the time was right to sit the three of us down and explain the facts of life. They felt – and now that I'm older, I understand the wisdom of doing so – that it was better if we heard it from them than from some misinformed elementary school loudmouth during recess.

Lee was disgusted. There was no way he was completing that act unless he had to, and the way he figured it, he would have to engage in this humiliation a total of three times, and three times only, because all he wanted was three children.

My brother, now 43, has three children. The rest of his family – well, mostly his older brother – assumes he has kept his word, and reminds him of his vow at every opportunity, especially those designed to extract the most embarrassment. Like, say, a book.

•

No other boy has ever awaited the arrival of his eighth birthday with more anticipation than I did.

When you were 8, you could play Little League in Ankeny. Uniforms. Teams. Coaches. Heaven. The first step toward what I assumed would be a meteoric rise straight to the major leagues, which I estimated would come somewhere between the eighth and ninth grades. Hold on, Bob Gibson,

I'm coming.

Dad was the assistant coach. The head coach for most of my Little League career was Gene Riley, a local banker whose son, Todd, was also on the team.

Gene was a fun-loving guy, but he stressed fundamentals. He taught us how to cover bunts, and why it was important to go from first to third on a base hit. He didn't just throw a ball on the field and let us play; he tried to teach us to love and appreciate the game. When we rode in his car, he'd crank up the music to get us fired up. "We're hummin' now!" was his favorite expression. I ate it up.

Todd remembers piling into his dad's red Chevy Malibu to travel to places like Polk City, Slater and Elkhart, with so many kids in the car that he wonders if a couple didn't ride in the trunk with the bats and balls.

"I couldn't wait to play," Todd says. "I would drown my glove in Glovolium the night before, just to be ready. When we took infield, my dad would have us field one between our legs, just to get the other team thinking.

"When I moved to Minneapolis, I played fast-pitch softball, and sometimes just out of the blue, I would look down the foul line and Dad would be leaning against the fence. He would leave work early in Waterloo and drive to Minneapolis to watch me play. After getting something to eat and talking ball, he would drive all the way back home. He loved baseball and softball.

"Even now, when I coach my boys, I'll yell out stuff like 'loosey goosey' or 'When you're hot, you're hot' " – two of his father's favorite phrases.

Gene Riley died a few years ago, but he left his son and his young players some indelible memories.

He was one of two men named Gene who figured prominently in my life. After games, I'd usually talk Dad into another game of catch in the backyard.

If our neighbor, Gene Scheffers, wasn't at the game – and he usually was – he'd show up in the backyard to get a pitch-by-pitch report from me.

On Friday nights, Gene would come over and we'd play cards or some other table games. Dad and Gene would disappear for a while, then show up with about three pounds of french fries from Henry's, a McDonald's rival back then. We'd then take a break to chow down on fries and Hi-C orange drink. I can still taste it.

I think I've made it pretty clear by now how much I admire my father, so I don't think it's any sign of disrespect to say that Gene Scheffers was another father figure to me, and a much-valued member of our family.

In fact, he was so important that this would be a good time to explain who he was and why everyone in our family loved him.

4
Gene

—

When I was in kindergarten, or perhaps first grade, I used to walk home after school. This was 1967, and it was a different era. Nowadays, most parents probably wouldn't let their young children walk two blocks unescorted.

One October afternoon as I was strolling home, I stopped by Gene Scheffers' home. I did this most days, actually. I'd step up on his stoop and look in the window to see if Gene was in his chair, and if he was, I'd knock on the door. I did this so many times I still have dreams about it.

Gene and my father became buddies – and that's the correct word, because they brought out the little boy in each other – when they worked together at Firestone. When my parents bought our house on Southwest Southlawn Drive in Ankeny, Gene bought a place about 12 houses away, on the same side of the street. It sounds farther away than it was. It always felt as if Gene was a neighbor.

He became a fixture at our house, eating dinner with us once or twice a week, stopping by to visit when Dad and I played catch. He bought us birthday and Christmas presents. When our parents took us to church on Christmas Eve, it was Gene who put the presents around our tree, to convince us that Santa had visited while we were out. He was like our favorite uncle.

On that afternoon in 1967, Gene was home, and he was watching the St. Louis Cardinals play the Boston Red Sox in the World Series. As I said, this was a different era. They actually played World Series games in the afternoon. The Cardinals, of course, were my favorite team, so Gene had no trouble persuading me to stay for a few outs.

A few outs turned into a few innings, and it was about that time that my mother began wondering what horrible fate had befallen me. She drove to the school; they told her that I had walked home, just like always. Mom and my brother walked the railroad tracks behind my house, searching for me, but I wasn't there. I was watching Lou Brock and Orlando Cepeda with Gene. Mom and Lee returned to the school. Still no Kent. While driving home, my brother spotted my head in Gene's house.

I'm not sure if Mom chewed out Gene or not – she wasn't the chewing-out type – but I'm sure she reminded Gene that the next time I visited, he might want to pick up the phone and give her a call, World Series or no World Series.

•

Gene was a lifelong bachelor. He had a sister, but we seemed to be part of his extended family. Mom said he once pointed out to her a woman with whom he had been in love, but it hadn't worked out and he never tried again.

It certainly didn't matter to me. Gene loved baseball, and he loved watching me play, and that was good enough. He was as much a fixture at my Little League games as my parents, and whenever I did something well, he beamed as brightly as they did.

I was good. I can see my parents wincing as they read this, because they certainly didn't raise me to brag, and I don't want to come across that way. But I knew I could play with anybody at that age. I didn't trash-talk or rub anybody's face in it. I tried to help the kids who weren't as good because, most of all, I wanted the team to win. I only point this out to show, at that stage in my life, it did not seem so fanciful to think that I would someday achieve my dream of playing professional baseball. If I was better than most kids when I was 10, why wouldn't I be better than most kids when I was 20?

I hit home runs. I routinely made the Ankeny all-star teams, which occasionally forced my parents to reschedule our summer vacation plans. We played games at the Four Mile Creek complex, near Interstate Highway 35 north of Des Moines, and there was just nothing better than getting a couple of hits in a game and buying a giant stick of taffy afterward.

Gene encouraged me at every opportunity. He was just as supportive to Debbie and Lee, but they weren't as interested in sports as I was, and Gene was a huge sports fan in a sports-crazy town.

I'll never forget the Christmas that he gave me a pair of Adidas gym shoes. Every kid had to have them, and I feared I would be left out. I was the sort of kid who would change my entire outfit if I saw something in the mirror that displeased me (I'm still this way), so you can imagine how overjoyed I was to have those popular shoes in my wardrobe. Mom told me that I couldn't wear them yet – this was winter, after all – but I put them in my duffel bag and put them on when I got to school.

I'm not sure if I told Gene about it, but I'd like to think he would have approved.

●

Dad, who was tall, and Gene, who was short, looked like Mutt and Jeff when they were together, but they shared an impish sense of humor.

I remember one time when they found a horn of some sort in the basement, and once outside discovered there was gunpowder in it. They dumped the gunpowder on the driveway and Gene used his cigarette lighter to ignite it. The explosion singed both men's eyebrows. As I said, they were little boys when together.

They pulled pranks on each other. Gene's house was a popular destination on Halloween because he always gave away full-size candy bars, not the miniatures. So Dad fashioned a costume out of a bed sheet and a mask and rang Gene's doorbell.

"Trick or treat," Dad said.

"Aren't you a little big to be trick or treating?" Gene asked.

"No," Dad replied, and then grabbed all the candy bars on the tray and stuffed them into his bag. When Gene started to protest, Dad pulled the mask off. Gene knew he had been had.

Another afternoon, Dad, Gene and I were going to raft on the Des Moines River from Jester Park, and then join the rest of our family for a picnic in Des Moines. I don't remember what happened, but we didn't reach Des Moines until 10 p.m., late enough that Mom called the police to see if any drowning victims had been pulled recently from the river. Nope, just three Iowa boys doing their best Huckleberry Finn imitations.

I'm sure in this cynical age there are those who might roll their eyes at the idea of a bachelor spending so much time with another couple and their children, and that's too bad. Because I associate Gene with good times, laughter, adventure and much love. He added as much to our lives as we did to his. Growing up wouldn't have been nearly as enjoyable without him.

•

One of the more exciting nights in my young life occurred one spring night in 1974, when I was 13. Our parents had joined three other couples who were celebrating their anniversaries. They were at the Adventureland Inn near Des Moines. My siblings and I were home alone (Debbie was as responsible as any parent).

Storms swept into the area, and the tornado sirens sounded. Debbie, Lee and I raced to the basement, and it sounded exactly like everyone always says it sounds – as if a train were passing overhead. We remained there, praying and talking, until our parents came home. Our home survived.

A few days later, at a grocery store parking lot, we went to get tetanus shots, a precautionary move because of all the tornado damage scattered about town. I passed out in my dad's arms, and they gave me the shot before I woke up. The sight of blood still makes me lightheaded.

•

Although baseball remained my true love, I was competitive enough to play all sports. If there was any sort of punting contest, free throw competition or track meet to be held, I would be there.

I played football as a boy. In eighth grade, we were divided into heavyweight and lightweight classes, and I was quarterback of the lightweights. In ninth grade, we combined the two teams, and I became a defensive back.

I didn't like getting hit, or hitting someone else, which are not the qualities one associates with a star football player (not to mention nearly fainting at the sight of blood), so that ended that portion of my athletic career. Besides, I didn't want to risk the sort of injury that might affect my baseball future. It's why I didn't play much golf then. I didn't want my golf swing to affect my baseball stroke.

Running the hurdles was my specialty in track. In eighth grade, I finished first in several meets, setting up a battle with a boy from Grinnell at the conference track meet in Ankeny. We had posted the two best times all season long, and I couldn't wait to face off against him.

I was too impatient, it turned out, because I jumped the gun twice and was disqualified. It was a terrible disappointment. It felt as if I had choked when it mattered the most. I didn't go out for track the next year, mostly because my left knee would swell up and turn black and blue from constantly slamming into the hurdle, but that loss stayed with me. It always seemed that I was agonizingly close – but not close enough – to achieving something great in sports.

High school awaited, and with it, the first tremors of doubt. Maybe I wasn't as good as I always thought I was.

5
Class of '80

From 1970, when I was in third grade, until 1980, the year I graduated from high school, my hometown of Ankeny swelled from 9,151 to 15,429 people.

Some of those new people were undoubtedly lured by the John Deere manufacturing plant, the town's largest employer. But most were drawn by the town's proximity to Des Moines, about 10 miles south. Ankeny offered city amenities with small-town neighborliness that parents with young children found irresistible. To this day, it remains a great place to raise a family.

And if it turns out that one or two of those children develop an affinity for sports – well, Ankeny is perfect. There seems to be some sort of athletic contest happening every night, on one of the many baseball diamonds, soccer fields and basketball courts. By 2009, Ankeny High School had captured 48 state championships in various boys' and girls' sports.

The flip side to this was, competition was fierce to crack one of the high school varsity teams. Only the most precocious talents earned varsity jerseys as sophomores. You were lucky to make the team, any team, as a senior.

So that became my lofty goal. I wanted to crack the Ankeny High School baseball team roster as a sophomore. My chances, I figured, were about 60-40. I was a decent hitter, but wasn't big or strong enough to send line drives off the outfield wall. My specialty was defense. I played shortstop and second base, and as Jack Buck might have said, I could vacuum the ball.

I wasn't the only sophomore with ambitious goals. Kevin Spitzig went on to play Division I football at the University of Iowa, and he was just as talented in baseball. Andy Crawford played first base at Iowa State University. Jim Ross would pitch for Grand View College; he became an academic All-American.

Kevin and Andy made the varsity as sophomores. I didn't, at least not at first.

I was crushed, but also determined. I'd just have to work harder.

●

I loved high school. If you asked my classmates, I think they'd say I got along with almost everyone. The jocks, the slackers, the stoners and the nerds, I counted all as friends. Even the teachers. I didn't smart off or cause problems. My parents weren't going to get any calls from the principal or police department because of any problem I had caused.

Their philosophy, which they repeated often, was simple: "We'll trust you until you do something not to earn that trust." I never tested them.

But one part of my personality must have made my parents want to tear their hair out. They were both teachers — Mom returned to the profession once Lee reached seventh grade — and both stressed education. It didn't work. I don't think I ever cracked a book to study in high school. My grades were decent enough — mostly A's and B's, the occasional C — but both knew I was capable of more.

I did, too, probably, but I always cared more about my batting average than my grade-point average. As long as I was eligible to compete, what did it matter? There were consequences to this behavior. I got kicked out of the National Honor Society because my grade-point average slipped below 3.0 (by 0.1, to be exact). But that didn't bother me all that much, either. The honor roll wasn't nearly as important to me as being selected to the Register's all-state baseball team.

I wasn't the only one who seemed to care more about sports than schoolwork. When I was in ninth grade, my parents received an urgent call from the algebra teacher, who wanted to meet with them. My goodness, they wondered, was Kent failing?

No, but I hadn't gone out for track. The algebra teacher, who also was the track coach, hoped my parents could change my mind. They were furious.

My parents tried to warn me. When I was younger, I knocked in the winning run in a kickball game. As I excitedly reported this to my father, he let me know that the game was far less important than the C that blemished the report card they had received in that day's mail.

"I'm glad you did well in the game," he said. "But we're going to talk about this."

Sure, Dad. Whatever you say.

A few years later, in high school, I remember Mom and Dad sitting me down and saying, "We're not going to badger you about it, but don't ever come back to us and say, 'I wish you had pushed me harder in school.' "

Don't worry, folks. I won't.

There were many times in the future that I would want to, but I never did.

•

When I wasn't playing in a game, or practicing for one, I was probably riding around town with Jim Ross and John Knudsen in Jim's Camaro, slurping Mountain Dew and eating CornNuts.

We were inseparable. Jim loved sports as much as I did. John moved to Ankeny in ninth grade, and because I was on the student council, I was asked to show him around. He was from Omaha and knew my cousin Todd. We hit it off right away.

Jim Ross and I took him under our wings, and we were our own gang. Jim now works at an ink manufacturing company in Des Moines. John is a special education teacher in Phoenix.

We didn't drink, which was probably unusual for that age and time, but it was an easy decision for me. I didn't want to let my parents down, and I certainly didn't want to be ruled ineligible. I couldn't imagine how horrible that would be.

I always considered myself a leader in high school. I led our church group, and I tried to set a good example for younger students. But one time I failed, and it still gnaws at me.

There was a student at Ankeny with special needs. One day, some of the kids began teasing him, as kids sometimes do. I watched it and did nothing. To this day, that disappoints me. I would eventually become a teacher and a principal, and I always felt I was an advocate for the special-needs students. There was a lot of bullying when we were kids, and usually I tried to stop it, but not that time.

Even now, I'd like to find him and tell him I'm sorry.

•

Don't get the wrong idea: I was a good kid, but I could still be a moody teenager.

One morning, when I was a senior, I didn't have to be at school until 10 a.m., and was looking forward to sleeping in. Mom walked into my room and told me it was time to get up.

"No."

"I said get up."

"No."

"Kent, get up."

I stormed out of that bed and mouthed off to her, in such a harsh way that it most likely surprised both of us. She kicked my leg (she was wearing slippers). I clenched my fist.

I immediately knew this was a mistake.

When Dad got home that night, he grabbed me by the shirt and pressed me against the wall. "Don't you ever do that again. Do you understand me?"

"Yes, sir."

And I never did.

I had disappointed myself and, worse, my parents. I'd rather have struck out with the bases loaded and the game on the line.

•

Mel Murken was the Ankeny varsity baseball coach. He was a wonderful guy, soft-spoken for the most part, but he could turn stern when the situation required it. He liked and trusted me. We always seemed to be prepared for every game. Just a good coach and a good man.

But he did something that sophomore year that surprised me and stunned the varsity team. I joined the varsity about midway through the season, but played sparingly. Then, right before our playoff run, he promoted me to starting shortstop. He never explained why – my defensive ability, I suspect – but it caused some resentment among the older players on the team, who felt loyalty toward the deposed player. I wasn't aware of any disgruntlement at the time, and it bothered me when I heard about it years later.

I played well, but we lost in the second round to Urbandale. My junior year, we reached the substate finals before losing to West Des Moines Dowling Catholic High School, one of our biggest rivals. We failed to reach the state tournament in Marshalltown my senior year as well, losing to Newton.

That year, I hit about .300 and was earning more attention for my defensive work. But would it be enough to earn one of those coveted slots on the Register's all-state team? Either first, second or third team would be fine with me. In my mind, I was good enough to make it.

But I didn't. Kevin Spitzig made the first team, and Andy Crawford made the second team. I received special mention all-state. Good, just not good enough.

•

I studied all my coaches, and if Mel Murken had a polar opposite in temperament and philosophy, it was Larry Ireland, the Ankeny varsity basketball coach.

Coach Ireland was a yeller. He screamed at us. His idea of motivation was to convince us that if we messed up, the wrath of the head coach was going to land on our heads. Nobody wanted that. Deep down, I loved playing for him. I had the same intensity to win burning inside me that he had; I had just trained myself to keep it inside. Coach Ireland let it out, and he prepared me well for what I would find later in college.

I played basketball all four years in high school, well enough that William Penn College (now William Penn University) in Oskaloosa recruited me to play basketball. During my junior year, we reached the state tournament, but lost in the semifinals to Dowling and Bobby Hansen, who would star at the University of Iowa and earn a National Basketball Association championship ring with Michael Jordan and the Chicago Bulls. I didn't play in any of our three games.

My senior year, I was the point guard, the floor leader, and I averaged about 10 points a game.

We were good, rated second in the state, and everyone looked forward to our upcoming game with No. 1-rated Des Moines Hoover High School. But in the game before the big one, while we were blowing out another team, I sprained my ankle severely.

I went through pregame warm-ups before the Hoover game, but I couldn't play. I sat on the bench as Hoover won by three or four points. I'll always wonder whether I could have made the winning difference, and I still have dreams – nightmares – of not getting to a big game in time.

We didn't advance to the state tournament that year. Good, just not good enough. This was becoming an unwelcome theme in my life. Jumping the gun in the hurdles ... not making the varsity team as quickly as I wanted as a sophomore ... not making one of the Register's all-state teams ... not being able to play against Hoover ... not winning a state championship in high school.

Perhaps I was just naive, or unwilling to accept reality, but my dream remained undeterred. I still planned and expected to play major-league baseball. All I needed was a chance, and that chance would be aided considerably if I could persuade a Division I college to offer me a scholarship.

6
Reality Bites
———————

I did not want to go to Waldorf College.

Nothing against Waldorf. It was a fine liberal arts college, about 100 miles north of Ankeny in Forest City, Iowa. It was affiliated with our church, the Evangelical Lutheran Church in America. My mother went there. My Aunt Karen went there. My sister Debbie went there.

It just wasn't the big time. I didn't think too many Waldorf baseball players had reached the major leagues. At the time, Waldorf was a junior college, a place you attended when you weren't good enough to play somewhere else. At least that's what I thought when I was an all-knowing high school senior.

My first preference was Arizona State University. During those summer vacations in Omaha, when my cousin Todd and I would go hunting for the elusive Bob Gibson, we would often attend the College World Series. And most years, it seemed, Arizona State would be there. They had two legendary coaches over the years, Bobby Winkles and Jim Brock, and a major-league roster's worth of talented players, including Reggie Jackson, Sal Bando, Bob Horner and Barry Bonds.

I could certainly envision myself as a Sun Devil. Next stop: the majors.

The trouble was, Arizona State and the other Division I colleges did not seem all that eager to recruit a good fielding, decent hitting infielder who had earned "special mention" all-state honors in Ankeny, Iowa.

It was terribly frustrating. The coaches at William Penn in Oskaloosa seemed eager to have me play basketball for them, but I didn't want to play basketball. I loved baseball, and I was going to be a baseball player. That was always the dream, and I wasn't about to give it up without a fight.

•

My first dose of reality came on a recruiting visit to Iowa State University, which still had a baseball program in 1980. The Cyclones weren't after me. They wanted my friend and classmate, Andy Crawford. I went along to keep Andy company and perhaps ignite some interest in my ability.

I took batting practice. Larry Corrigan, the ISU coach, was kind enough to say he had seen me play in high school, and he was complimentary. He said I was a good defensive player, but I didn't hit well enough yet to play for them. Why not, he said, go to a junior college for two years, work on your hitting, and come see me again after that?

It was a slender reed to hang on to, but I had little else. At my parents' urging, I had applied to Waldorf, and had been accepted. But I was still hoping that a Division I coach might take a chance on me.

No such luck. I was headed to Waldorf, which offered me a $200 scholarship to play baseball. Wow. What a can't-miss phenom I had turned out to be.

●

You remember how, when you were a teenager, and had the entire world figured out, something would happen to quickly remind you how little you actually knew?

Such was the case the first day I set foot on the Waldorf College baseball diamond.

Those guys were good. Really good. The team was ranked 13th in the country among junior colleges. Three of our four pitchers would be selected by professional teams in the spring draft. Todd Oakes would pitch in the San Francisco Giants' organization; he's now the pitching coach for the University of Minnesota. My teammates were as committed as I was. We all felt we had something to prove.

This was serious baseball, on a team that returned all of its starters. During the first intrasquad game, I batted against Mark Danker, who would become a good friend. It took one pitch from him to realize I wasn't in high school anymore. I'd either learn to hit or learn to play something else. Like Monopoly.

I was in luck. Waldorf's head coach, Jim Hayden, was a proponent of the Charley Lau theory of hitting. Lau was a former American League catcher and hitting coach whose students included George Brett and Hal McRae. Pretty good resume.

Lau had written a popular book, "The Art of Hitting .300," in which he said a hitter should balance his weight on his back foot before striding into the ball, maintain flat hands through the ball and release the top hand after making contact, following through with the lower hand.

It was a revelation. I was suddenly spraying line drives across the field, and surprising even myself by knocking the ball out of the park on occasion. I'll always wonder whether I might have been more attractive to a Division I baseball coach had I discovered Charley Lau a year earlier, but I was having too much fun at Waldorf, watching my batting average climb, to waste much time pining for what might have been.

I hit .340 my freshman year, splitting second-base duties with a sophomore. I had never hit that well in high school.

The dream was alive.

•

Coach Hayden could have been a Marine drill sergeant in another life. He told us he had spies in area bars, and we'd better not be caught in one. We believed him.

The players feared him, but I wasn't intimidated. I had played for Coach Ireland, so I knew how to deal with intense coaches. You listen to what they're saying, not how loudly they're shouting it or what names they are calling you as they shout it. I always felt I could have played for someone like Bob Knight, the legendary basketball coach. If a coach sincerely cared about helping me get better, I didn't care how much or how long he yelled at me. Not everyone appreciates that approach, I realize, but it worked for me.

Waldorf was perfect for me. There were about 300 students – Ankeny High School had three times that many – and you could get to know them. The school had good football and wrestling teams, a wonderful fine arts department and a strong women's athletics program. I got along with everyone, just like in high school.

One of the best things about being there was that it was close enough to Grandpa and Grandma Lee's home – they had moved to Story City – that they could watch most of my games. They might show up anywhere, and it was always a treat. One time, I hit a grand slam, and Grandpa Lee was so excited he called my folks, then made them promise not to let on that they knew when I called later that night.

My parents attended as many games as they could, but both were still teaching. They were able to make the game we played in Cedar Rapids, at the ballpark used by the Kernels, now the Class A affiliate of the California Angels. I hit a home run, rounded the bases, then jumped up and gave a high-five to Dad, who was sitting in the first row behind our dugout.

The best part about playing sports, and doing well, is all the people you can bring along for the ride. My parents and grandparents were enjoying every minute of it. So was I.

•

Coach Hayden made us a deal: If we won the conference tournament, he'd let us go out to the bars and drink without penalty (most of us could legally drink back then). This was a little like having the surgeon general offer you a carton of cigarettes, and we enthusiastically accepted the offer.

We won the tournament. Barely. We were much better than any other conference school, and should have won each game by 10 runs. Instead, we played sloppy, uninspired baseball and were lucky to win.

Afterward, Coach Hayden ripped into us. You might have won, he said, but you played like crap. There would be no celebrating this ugly effort. He revoked our party passes.

About 10 of us went out anyway, hoping that his network of spies didn't reach bars in the greater Mason City area. Just like in the tournament, we got lucky.

Our hope of capturing a national title died in the regional tournament, when we were upset.

Later that week, Coach Hayden invited us to a bar in Forest City, and he supplied the keg. That by itself should have warned us that something big was about to happen.

"Well, guys, I'm leaving Waldorf."

I'm not sure what happened. We were stunned, but probably should have expected it. One of the problems with intense coaches is that they burn brightly, but quickly, and tend to singe some of the people around them. I think the Waldorf administration decided that the baseball team might benefit from a calmer captain at the helm, but you'll never hear me say an unkind word about Coach Hayden. He revived my career.

●

Sometime that season, I made a triumphant return to Ankeny, where I was prepared to regale my friend Gene Scheffers with my newfound hitting prowess.

Gene had been diagnosed with stomach cancer the year before, when I was a high school senior, so he usually wasn't well enough to make any of my college games, although I'm sure he would have enjoyed them. I always made sure to stop in and see him whenever I was home.

He was my buddy, my ally, my confidant. I could talk to him about things I might not share with my parents. So I didn't think twice about plugging a chaw of tobacco in my lip, one of the habits I had picked up along with a decent hitting stroke at Waldorf.

Gene didn't say anything, but he certainly noticed. I don't know whether it was his cancer or the fact that he never could break a lifetime addiction to cigarettes, but as soon as I left, he called my parents and ratted me out.

I know he had my best interests at heart, but Gene triggered an uncomfortable confrontation with my parents, who of course were disappointed, if not horrified. They made me promise to quit. I promised, and some days was even able to keep that promise.

I forgave Gene for what struck me then as a breach of trust, but I never chewed tobacco in front of him again. Nor did I tell him that, like most college boys, I had developed an appreciation for the occasional sip of Budweiser.

•

The next season, our baseball coach was Mark Dykema. If Waldorf administrators wanted Coach Hayden's mirror opposite, they got it. He was so laid back that some of the players walked all over him. We weren't the most disciplined team. Coach Hayden would have killed us – that's no exaggeration – for some of the stunts we pulled with Coach Dykema.

When Coach Hayden left, many of my fellow freshmen ballplayers decided to leave as well. I'm not sure Coach Dykema got as much out of us as Coach Hayden would have, but we still played hard and finished 22-22. We didn't qualify for the regional tournament.

I learned something important that year: You can't be friends with your players, like Coach Dykema had tried to be with us. You can support your players, and laugh with them, but there needs to be a clear line of authority when it's time to get the work done.

Although the team struggled, I continued to play well. I hit .330, with seven home runs.

But my days at Waldorf were numbered, and so, it appeared, was my opportunity to play Division I baseball. No big-time recruiters came after me, and I'm still not sure why. I thought I had played well enough to at least attract a nibble. Maybe they had the same shortsighted image of Waldorf that I had as a high school senior.

Mostly, I think, I was a victim of circumstance. Coach Hayden seemed to have a lot of contacts at the bigger schools; a recommendation from him might have been enough for a Division I scholarship. I'm not sure Coach Dykema had those kinds of relationships, or even considered it part of his job.

Iowa State expressed no interest. I could have walked on there or at the University of Iowa, or perhaps another larger school, but that's a little like trying to strike it rich by winning the lottery.

My parents always told me to keep a backup plan handy, and now it appeared they were right. I had to finally accept reality: I was never going to play professional baseball. It was a crushing self-admission. This may sound like hyperbole, but it's absolutely true: From the time I was old enough to play catch with Mom in my playpen, I had truly never considered doing anything else. I felt like a hopeless failure. It was worse than that, actually. I felt foolish, as if I had spent my life chasing a mirage.

About the best I could do now was follow the same track many of my family members had taken and enroll at Luther College in Decorah. I could play two more years of college baseball while I charted a new future.

It was time to face facts. Time to grow up. No more kids' games.

Except it didn't work out that way. A combination of factors – including the realization that my baseball-playing dream was over – merged to produce the worst, darkest year of my life.

7

The Lost Season

————————————

The summer of 1982 represented a transition for me, and not a particularly pleasant one. I had just graduated from Waldorf College, and was preparing to enter Luther College in Decorah, the northeast Iowa school to which my Grandpa Lee had dreamed of returning. He and two uncles preceded me there; my brother, Lee, would follow me.

It appeared, on the surface, that my future was mapped out, but I was adrift. The realization that I wouldn't be playing professional baseball left me unsettled. But my future wasn't my biggest worry in July 1982.

Gene Scheffers was dying.

He had decided to end treatments for the stomach cancer, and his health subsequently declined. I tried to see him as often as possible, taking him a milk shake, which was about the only thing he could stand to eat.

One of my milk shakes was still on the table, melting, on the day he died.

Dad got the call that an ambulance was at his house. When he arrived, he met Dr. R.C. Wooters, the kindhearted Polk County medical examiner who had pronounced Gene dead. Dad explained Gene's unique role in our family's life.

Why don't you bring the children here so they can say goodbye? Dr. Wooters asked.

It was one of the most emotional experiences of my life. My eyes still fill with tears thinking about it. Grandpa Stock had died in 1977, my freshman year in high school, but this was different. Gene was a part of my daily life. It felt as if my father had died.

"The kids were just devastated," my mother says.

But Dr. Wooters was a wise man, and over the years it has helped me considerably to have seen Gene in his house one last time. I have never regretted it.

That doesn't mean I handled it well.

●

I've portrayed my life to this point like a series of rosy scenes from a 1960s sitcom, and it's true. It was a wonderful childhood, full of warm and loving memories with supportive friends and family members.

But it probably left me in less than an ideal position to deal with life's inevitable sadness, failures and disappointments. To me, Gene's death was another blow, like the end of my baseball-playing dream, that suggested my happy-go-lucky youth was over.

My faith had taught me that God had a plan for me, and I had always believed it. Now I wondered. My life certainly wasn't going in the direction I once had anticipated. Losing Gene was another reminder.

Sure, some of it, maybe a lot of it, was self-pity. I was always a sensitive kid. I'd get so homesick when I stayed with my cousin Todd in Omaha as a boy that my aunt would have to put my mother on the phone to console me. When I was in high school, I hated confrontations or any sort of turmoil, and would try to serve as peacemaker.

I knew Gene was sick, and his death wasn't a shock, but my emotions overpowered me nonetheless. For a long time, longer than was good for me, I was upset, angry and depressed that Gene had died. He was only 51 years old. It wasn't fair.

Probably the best way to describe what happened next is that I spiraled into a rebellious rage. I drank more than I ever had before. When I returned to Luther that fall, I skipped classes. I'd always been able to get by academically with a minimal amount of effort; I figured I'd do even less now. I simply didn't care.

Baseball season wouldn't begin until second semester, a few months away, so I had little structure to my life. And there's no better way to make instant friends in college than to be willing to party with them. I made lots of new friends.

Later in my life, after I became a middle school principal, I often told undisciplined students that actions have consequences, whether we realize it at the time or not.

It was a lesson I learned when first-semester grades were released.

My grade-point average was 1.28. To remain eligible, a minimum grade-point average of 2.0 was required.

When the Luther College baseball team took the field the next spring, I would not be with them.

I had gotten exactly what I deserved.

•

I was home, in Ankeny, over Christmas break when the grades arrived.

My parents were disappointed, obviously, but also supportive. I think in the back of their minds they knew my lax study habits were going to catch up with me eventually. They had done their best to warn me. To their credit, they didn't remind me of their many lectures. They had been proven right once again.

But no baseball? Even I didn't think it had gotten that bad. I figured I'd pull out a 2.0 grade-point average and still remain eligible. I had played baseball every spring since I was 8 years old. I wasn't sure what I would do with myself.

I sat on my mother's lap, like a little boy.

"I'm blanking stupid," I said, uttering a word I had never said before or since in her presence.

She didn't blink.

"No, you're not. You just don't try."

She was right.

•

When I returned to Luther, a trip to the woodshed awaited me, in the form of a visit with Chris Moorcroft, my adviser.

I don't remember how she phrased it, but her message went something like: What are you going to do, Kent? Are you staying or going? Are you going to turn it around?

It was the kick in the rear I needed. Coach Ireland and Coach Hayden would have been proud of her. She had unleashed my competitive spirit.

I'm not going anywhere, I told her. And I will turn this around.

If this were a movie, we'd quickly cut to the scene where I solved some inscrutable math formula that completely altered the way we view the universe. It didn't quite happen that way. Instead, I began studying, aiming for B's and C's instead of D's and F's. My grade-point average began inching up. Slowly but steadily.

It would be many years before I gained any confidence as a student, but when the 1984 baseball season began, I was a member in good, not great, academic standing at Luther College.

●

I'm still not entirely sure what happened to me. It almost felt as if I had gone into some sort of shock. Or like a train that had gotten knocked off its path by a lightning bolt.

But I was lucky. My parents had shown me the right path. There's a saying that I appreciate: Prepare the child for the path, not the path for the child. I had veered off the path, but thanks to them, I knew where it was. I could find my way back.

Once again, baseball gave me a direction. I had one more year of eligibility left, in 1984, and I planned to make the most of it.

The Luther coach was Paul Solberg. I'm not sure whether he was the most knowledgeable baseball expert, whether he knew where each player should be positioned on every play, but he'll always be in my personal Hall of Fame as a human being. He was a father figure to many of us. He cared more about our success off the baseball diamond than whether we got a key hit in a big game. He was exactly what I needed at the time, and I admired him tremendously. Still do.

I had saved my best for last. I led the team in hitting, batting .415 in the conference, .395 overall, and was named the all-conference shortstop. We lost in the Division III regional finals that year – continuing my streak of never winning a championship – but my personal life was back on track. Like my mother and father, I had decided to become a teacher.

If I couldn't play baseball, I could coach it.

●

Another devastating personal loss occurred in the summer of 1984. Grandpa Lee died after a brief battle with colon cancer.

I handled it more maturely than Gene's death, but it was still terribly painful. I remember one weekend that spring, when Grandpa worsened and they called the family together. I borrowed a car from a cousin in Ossian, Iowa, which was nine miles from Decorah, and drove all the way to Mary Greeley Medical Center in Ames, about three hours away, to see him. It was our last time together.

He knew I had made first-team all-conference. Even in his dying moments, he was still my biggest fan, and there have been many moments in my life since then when I have thought how great it would be to share them with Grandpa Lee.

●

I feel the same way about Gene Scheffers as I do about Grandpa Lee.

For most of Gene's life, or at least since he had become friends with our family, he bought savings bonds for my brother, sister and me. He didn't tell anybody about it, not even my parents. We didn't find out about it until his will was opened.

I don't remember the amount. It wasn't a fortune by any means – Gene was not a wealthy man – but it doesn't matter. It demonstrates the kind of person he was. Even after he was gone, Gene was still looking after us. It's difficult to imagine having a more loyal friend.

I'll miss him and Grandpa Lee forever.

8
Coach Stock

Because of the semester I had spent partying and skipping class, I needed a fifth year at Luther College to earn enough credits and complete the student teaching assignment that was required for a teaching certificate.

That extra year turned out to be greatly beneficial. By the time I left Luther, I knew exactly what I wanted to do. I wanted to teach, and I wanted to coach baseball.

Coach Solberg gave me my first taste of coaching. I was one of his student assistants in the winter of 1985 (my eligibility to play had ended), and I enjoyed everything about it. I had the same duties as an assistant coach, working with the hitters and infielders.

I liked hitting grounders. I liked giving tips on the proper fielding position for a double play. I liked – loved, actually – seeing an average hitter become better because of something I had told him. All of that time I had spent as a boy, studying the game, watching coaches, listening to Jack Buck or Mike Shannon explain the proper way to play, reading Charley Lau's tips on hitting, may not have gotten me to the major leagues. But it was the perfect training to be a baseball coach.

My only problem was time. I didn't have enough of it.

When baseball games began that spring, I was student teaching at Waukon High School. I taught ninth-grade general business with Fran Luther and high school accounting with Don Pothost. Both were patient with me, and I knew that I had chosen the right profession.

But Waukon is about 20 miles away from Decorah, the home of Luther, and I just didn't have enough time to give both the student teaching job and the baseball coaching position the full attention they required. I had to make a decision.

For the first time in my life, I chose academics over baseball. I told Coach Solberg I needed to leave the team, and he understood. But I had little doubt that I would be back on a baseball field again before long.

•

I was back even quicker than I had anticipated.

After graduating from Luther that May, I returned home to Ankeny to begin searching for a job. I figured I'd probably earn some spending cash working at a hotel restaurant, which is what I had done in previous summers.

But Dad had another idea. He was teaching at East High School in Des Moines then, and was talking to Chuck Sutherland, the head baseball coach. Coach Sutherland needed someone to coach the ninth-grade team and serve as his assistant with the varsity team that summer. Would I be interested?

Oh, baby.

I was only 23 years old, and probably looked younger than half the freshman team, but I wasn't intimidated. In fact, I felt as if I was born for it.

But I had a problem. A total of 45 boys had gone out for ninth-grade baseball. Coach Sutherland, to his credit, had a no-cut policy. But there were only 20 uniforms. I had to decide who would play in games and who wouldn't.

It was an agonizing decision. It reminded me of my own youth, when boys were split between the A and B teams. Nobody, most of all me, wanted to be on the B team. At East, I could rotate uniforms, so everyone got at least one chance to be in a game, but I knew I was going to make at least half the boys unhappy.

I tried to explain to them that all were important members of the team, and I meant it. Baseball is a team effort. Every player matters. The batboys, too. As a coach, you've got to make sure everyone feels important. Playing favorites is incredibly destructive. It builds resentment among teammates who need to trust and believe in each other when the game is on the line.

Whitey Herzog, the former Cardinals manager, once said he tried to talk to every one of his players every single day, just to see how they were doing, but more important, to let them know that he hadn't forgotten about them. I tried to do the same thing that summer, whether a boy was starting in the next game or not.

Despite my best efforts, all but five of those 25 boys quit. But I kept my word, and made sure those other five were rotated on the team and were given a chance to play.

Years later, I heard that one of the five boys who stuck it out that summer made all-conference when he was a senior. That was another lesson I've tried to impart to my players over the years: Don't ever quit. Surprising things can happen when you don't.

●

Speaking of surprises, I'll bet Dal Maxvill, who was then the general manager of the St. Louis Cardinals, wasn't expecting the letter of application that landed on his desk about that time.

A Luther College graduate with no previous coaching experience at the professional level, but with a burning desire to learn, thought he'd explore the possibility of getting a coaching job in the Cardinals organization. Any coaching job, no matter how far down in the organizational food chain.

Maxvill, a former Cardinals shortstop, wrote me a generous thanks-but-no-thanks response.

Look, I know it seems ludicrous for me to think the Cardinals were going to offer me a position, but I will give myself credit for this much: I've always had the courage to take a risk. The easy thing in life is to assume that you'll be turned down, not get the job, not make the team. Why bother? But that's never been part of my nature, and I've been rewarded many more times than I've been rejected.

•

That summer with Coach Sutherland was a joy. He had a cool, calm and collected style that put his players at ease. He reminded me of my father – he commanded respect instead of demanding it. I learned from him about the pace of a game and how to handle yourself on the diamond.

But I knew this was a temporary job. I still needed to begin my teaching career.

I sent my resume to several schools – I hoped to stay in Iowa – and my first interview was for the high school business teaching and head girls' basketball coaching job in Parkersburg. I wanted to coach baseball, but I needed to get the teaching job first.

The interview went well, but the job went to somebody else. I wasn't depressed. I figured it might take 10 interviews to finally land something.

I got lucky. Jim Thornton, the high school principal at Waukon, where I had student taught, was good friends with Rich Hobart, the superintendent at Belle Plaine High School. Because of Thornton's recommendation, I got an interview in Belle Plaine.

It lasted two hours. At the end, Rich asked me some coaching questions, then told me I'd hear from him.

He called a few days later: Would I like to teach high school business and coach the junior high boys' basketball and junior high girls' volleyball teams in Belle Plaine?

Absolutely.

There was just one problem: I knew nothing about volleyball. It was one of the few sports I had never played or had much interest in.

I thought the good Lord was playing tricks on me.

You want to be a coach, Kent? OK, I'll make you a coach. A junior high girls' volleyball coach.

What had I gotten myself into?

9
Belle Plaine

Wouldn't you know it? About two weeks after I accepted the Belle Plaine position, an administrator at Waldorf College called me: Would I be interested in being the head baseball coach?

That would have been a great job. I'd be coaching my favorite sport, baseball, at a school that took baseball seriously. Despite my youthful apprehension, I had grown to love Waldorf. I made friends there whom I still cherish. Some of my favorite memories were made there. The job sounded perfect.

But I had given Belle Plaine my word. I didn't want to begin my teaching career by reneging and putting the school in the position of having to scramble to replace me. Once again, baseball would have to wait.

Belle Plaine is a community of about 2,900 people, about 40 miles west of Cedar Rapids. It has a golf course, movie theater and bowling alley, which sold the best greasy hamburgers I've ever eaten. The Lincoln Cafe served a terrific Sunday brunch, and the Pizza Hut there was the setting for one of the most important meetings of my life.

Belle Plaine would be my home for the next 13 years.

Have you ever strolled into a cafe in a small town where you were a stranger? Seen the faces look up and stare at you curiously, as if you might have pink hair, or had somehow forgotten to put on pants that morning?

That's sort of how I felt my first few months there. I felt as if I was being checked out, and I was. They waited to see whether the young outsider would prove worthy. Once they accepted you, you were a townie for life. I eventually gained their trust and friendship, but it took a while.

Impressing the locals was not my first order of business when I arrived in Belle Plaine in the fall of 1985.

I still needed to learn the rules of volleyball.

●

Well, I figured, if I was going to coach junior high girls' volleyball, I'd try to be the best volleyball coach I could be.

My brother, Lee, had played the sport at Luther, so he offered a quick tutorial. I bought volleyball books. I attended volleyball clinics. I studied the game the way I had studied baseball as a boy.

And – this surprised me – I became enchanted with the sport. There's a lot more involved than smacking a ball back and forth over a net, I certainly learned that.

That first season, my junior high girls seemed more interested in cheering than playing, and I'm not sure how much coaching I was able to accomplish. But we competed well, and I enjoyed being with them.

The next summer, while golfing with Rich Hobart, the superintendent who had hired me, he told me the varsity volleyball coach had resigned. Would I like to take over the varsity?

I gulped and accepted.

•

Coaching volleyball was a blast, but that represented only half of my coaching duties. I also was the junior high boys' basketball coach.

That was not a blast, I'm sad to report, at least at first.

Belle Plaine had always been a wrestling school, but the basketball players weren't the problem. I was terrible.

Looking back, I think it was a blessing that I knew zilch about volleyball when I began coaching. I didn't have any preconceived notions. I was learning at such an elementary level myself that I could better explain to the girls what I wanted them to do. They were learning the fundamentals along with me.

But I had played basketball, and been a starter in high school. As I indicated earlier, I liked playing, but the sport held no magical spell over me. I could take it or leave it. As a result, I don't think I ever developed a simple, clear, easily understandable system for coaching. I just sort of expected the boys to know how to play by instinct. After all, that's how I played.

So I yelled a lot. I became a junior version of Coach Ireland, but at least he had many years of basketball expertise to convey with his shouting. I got technical fouls called on me in games. I basically made a fool of myself.

Perhaps it was the memory of my dad pulling me aside during a Little League game, warning me not to embarrass myself or my family, that led to an epiphany. Screaming and shouting wasn't my coaching style. All it did was make my players nervous. It wasn't the kind of coach I wanted to be.

I calmed down, and forced myself to keep whatever frustration I felt locked inside. I coached junior high and varsity boys' basketball in Belle Plaine for nine seasons. Our teams were average, at best, and I can't say it was the most fun I ever experienced in sports. But I could live with it, and apparently the administration could, too, because something else was occurring at this same time.

Belle Plaine was becoming a volleyball power.

●

Other coaches had told me that there was a big difference between coaching boys and girls, and I found that to be true.

With boys, you could criticize them individually. They might not like it, but often it would inspire them to play harder, just to prove that you were wrong. With girls, if you criticized them individually too often, they would turn on you. You'd lose them.

I'd like to think the Belle Plaine girls' volleyball team saw the best of me. Instead of yelling at them, I encouraged them. Instead of pointing out where they had fallen short, I complimented them for what they had done right. If I needed to get on them, I got on them as a team, not as individuals.

We were learning together. My first year as head coach was only the third year that Belle Plaine had offered volleyball. If I could get them on my side, I discovered, they'd do anything for me. In fact, one year, coming out of a huddle, we'd shout in unison, "Through the wall!" – which meant that if I asked them to run through a wall, they'd trust me enough to do it. And that team would have.

This was the time in my life when I realized I was a good coach. I had tried to take the best qualities of the coaches in my life –and the coaches whose books I had read, like John Wooden – and had merged them with my own personality.

Not to pat myself on the back too hard, but I think I had learned the sport well enough to train the girls and put them in a position to succeed.

I've always believed that should be the first goal of any coach, or boss, in sports or out. If you want to succeed, give your players a chance to do so.

In only a few years, I had gone from knowing nothing about volleyball to being able to take a girl who couldn't walk and chew gum at the same time and transform her into a middle blocker. I had learned the great joy of helping young athletes get better. Being a coach does not supply the same ego jolt as hitting a grand-slam home run. The satisfaction is deeper; you're part of something bigger than yourself. And you're not just part of it, you're leading it.

Before long, it all came together.

We started winning.

●

In the fall of 1989, my third year as the varsity volleyball coach, we won in the first round of the district tournament. The next night, Norway would play Mount Vernon, and we would face the winner. I drove to Mount Vernon to scout the game.

I had a notebook in my hand as I approached the bleachers. There, high in the corner, sat Jim Van Scoyoc. His daughter played for Norway.

He didn't know me, but I certainly knew who Jim Van Scoyoc was. All those years of studying the Register had provided a nearly complete biography. At that time, in 1989, he had coached the Norway High School baseball team to 11 state titles. He had sent several players to professional baseball. He was as good as it gets.

I headed up the bleachers, taking a seat about 15 feet away. As the matches began, I moved a little bit closer to him, then closer, then still closer. I felt like a stalker, but he didn't say anything. Finally, I was close enough that he could hear me.

I took a deep breath. I've told you that I've always been the kind of guy who is willing to take a risk. This was, for me, a huge risk. The last thing I wanted to do was intrude on him or irritate him. It would be like tempting Bob Gibson to tell me to get lost. On the other hand, would I ever have this opportunity again?

Remember that moment when you were a kid, standing on the diving board, terrified to jump but also too committed to turn back? Sometimes you've just got to jump.

Here, in the Mount Vernon gym, I jumped.

10
Joining the Legend

———————————

I extended my hand.

"Coach Van Scoyoc?" I said. "I'm Kent Stock of Belle Plaine. It's an honor to meet you."

By the end of the evening, I had concluded that Jim Van Scoyoc might have been the first person I ever met who loved baseball even more than I did.

We hit it off immediately, sitting on those Mount Vernon bleachers, watching his daughter and the Norway volleyball team win their match. We talked the entire night, about baseball, volleyball, coaching, kids. I'm not sure I did much scouting.

Jim is a few years older, and I immediately settled into a position comfortable for me, that of a student learning from a mentor. He was like Gene Scheffers, Gene Riley, Mel Murken, Jim Hayden and Paul Solberg, older men with whom I had bonded simply because I wanted to know as much about baseball as they did.

With Jim, that was going to be impossible; I'd settle for knowing 10 percent. Heading into the 1990 baseball season, the man had won 11 state titles in a town of 586 people. Think of that. Maybe you'd luck out in a small town and get a batch of athletic kids who were good enough to compete for a state title for one year, but finding enough talent in a town that size to compete, and win, year after year after year? Jim Van Scoyoc was a miracle worker.

At least that's what I thought before I got to know him. What I discovered later was that there was no magic about it. He and his teams just outworked everyone else.

As the conversation continued that night, and we talked about Norway's upcoming season, Jim told me he needed to replace his assistant coach, who had resigned.

Once again, I jumped.

Summoning as much courage as I could muster, I said, "Coach, would you accept an application from a guy from Belle Plaine?"

"You bet," he said. "Send a letter of application to my athletic director."

"Who's your athletic director?"

Jim flashed me a grin I would come to see often, when he knew he had gotten me.

"My athletic director is Jim Van Scoyoc."

●

I returned home that night, wrote the letter, and mailed it to him.

Two nights later, my volleyball team played Norway in the district finals. The winner would advance to substate play. They smoked us, three games to none. Well, I figured, Jim Van Scoyoc couldn't have been too impressed with my coaching ability that night. Why would he want a losing volleyball coach to serve as his assistant?

The next week, he called and said he'd like to meet me at the Pizza Hut in Belle Plaine for an interview.

We talked for three hours. I listened mostly, as he talked about life, baseball, his coaching philosophy, theories, whom we knew in common, our favorite baseball players and teams.

He talked about loyalty. To him, loyalty was everything. But not just loyalty to friends and family members. He talked about remaining loyal to yourself, to what you believe in. Once he believed in something, or someone, that was it.

In another era, he might have been a cowboy, John Wayne or Clint Eastwood, the guy who remains calm and steady when gunfire erupts. If I ever asked Jim a question, I knew I was going to get a straight answer. There was no hype to the man. I sometimes think that's one of the reasons he was drawn to baseball. When you're standing in the batter's box, waiting for the pitch, you can't talk or fake your way out of it. You can either hit the ball or you can't. Phonies don't last very long.

Sitting there in the Pizza Hut, I was in awe. I'm not sure Jim was well known nationally, but he was a legend to me. I couldn't believe my good luck just visiting with him, not to mention potentially coaching with him.

It's hard to describe, but it felt as if I'd known him my entire life. We just clicked.

He didn't mention my baseball coaching experience, which consisted of supervising a ninth-grade team one summer. If he had any doubts about me, he didn't express them. I think he knew that my motives were sincere. All I wanted to do was learn from him.

At the end of the night, he offered me the assistant coaching job. In the spring of 1990, I would have a front-row seat in baseball heaven. I would help Jim Van Scoyoc coach the Norway High School baseball team.

It was one of the happiest nights of my life.

•

I've heard the question hundreds of times: What was it about that little town that produced so much great baseball?

First, it was the tradition. Old-timers there talked about playing competitive baseball in the 1920s. In 1965, the year after Bernie Hutchison became coach, the high school won its first title.

"I used to get a kid off a bike so we would have enough to play," Hutchison said in a newspaper interview. "But once you win, everybody's kind of on the bandwagon and it gets to be a tradition."

Norway won two spring titles and five fall titles under Hutchison. Van Scoyoc won his first championship in the fall of 1972.

But it wasn't just high school kids who played and won. Boys played in leagues from third grade until they were too old to play on the adult town team.

Spend any time there, and you were sure to hear about Max Elliott, who became a professional softball player in New Zealand, or Mike Boddicker, who struck out 1,122 batters in high school before becoming a major-leaguer, or pitcher John Kuester, who went 42-0 and won four state titles, or Dick McVey, a pitcher who helped Norway win a title in the spring of 1967, before schools were divided by size. In the final that year, Norway beat Mason City. Talk about David upsetting Goliath.

Perhaps they played so much baseball in Norway because there weren't many distractions. Norway didn't have a swimming pool or a video game parlor, but there was a baseball diamond. By the time I arrived, they didn't even have a grocery store anymore, just a gas station. After games, boys would gather there, around the soda pop machine.

Finally, and perhaps most important, a youngster growing up in Norway learned, from his grandparents, parents, older brothers and older friends, how to play the game right. Norway boys knew how to field a ground ball properly before they learned the alphabet. They knew when to take an extra base, and when not to. They were learning why it was important to hit the cutoff man when other boys were more concerned with reading Mad magazine. Playing fundamentally sound baseball was part of the town's DNA.

I took a notebook with me to the first practice, and was immediately surprised. There were probably as many fans in the stands for a practice as some towns draw for games.

The players seemed to reflect their head coach, serious and professional. There wasn't much goofing off when Jim Van Scoyoc was on the field. Don't get me wrong – it wasn't basic training in the Marine Corps – but there was a sense of purpose from the opening drill.

That first practice, Jim told me to hit fungoes to the outfield. I grabbed a bat for the first time in a while, and paid the price. My hands were soft. The blisters came quickly, but I ignored them. I can't imagine the look that would have appeared on Jim's face had I told him, "Sorry, Coach, can't do it anymore. My hands sting." My arms would have to fall off before that was going to happen.

●

Those were long, happy days. I usually arrived in Norway about 8 a.m., raking the diamond, getting the field ready. I invested my heart and soul into being Jim's assistant. Sometimes we'd go to the Amana Colonies for lunch. After games, his wife, Chick, would cook supper for us, and we'd talk baseball some more, long into the night.

I'll never forget my first dinner at his house, when he walked in and gave his wife a big kiss.

"Why, Jim," I said. "You do have a heart."

Beneath that no-nonsense exterior was a true softy, especially around his wife and daughter. I've heard that if a youngster showed up at his house, Jim would invariably give him a box of baseball cards to take home (he has a huge card collection).

Jim told me he wanted me to be an extra set of eyes and ears on the field for him. I should feel free to speak my mind. If I thought a pitcher was getting tired, I should tell him.

One of the things he told me was, "I hear everything you're saying. If I don't do what you suggest, it's not because I didn't hear you, it's because I chose to do something else. Don't ever stop talking to me and don't ever stop telling me what you're seeing, but don't say it twice."

That summer was like getting a master's degree in baseball. But Jim Van Scoyoc wasn't just the best professor a young coach could want. He became a lifelong friend.

•

The Norway baseball diamond sat in the southwest corner of town. Beyond left field was the gray steeple of St. Michael's Catholic Church. The American flag flew beyond the fence in center field. Every so often, a train would rumble in the distance beyond right field. Legend had it that Hal Trosky once hit a ball that landed on the highway and bounced over the tracks.

We had a very good team in 1990. As usual, Norway played some of the biggest schools in the state during the regular season and won its share of the games.

As the season progressed, I noticed that Jim would put players in different positions, or sometimes bring a rarely used pitcher into a close game (in Norway, every boy was a pitcher until he proved otherwise). He was testing them to see who could handle the pressure and who would wilt. Everything

– from the tough schedule to the lineup – was a gut check designed by him to put the team in the best possible position come state tournament time.

Junior Tyson Kimm emerged as a star that season and he's a perfect example of how the Norway legacy was passed from one generation to the next. His father, Bruce, a catcher, was a star on Norway teams in the 1960s, and that summer was a coach for the San Diego Padres.

Once again, Norway advanced to the Class 1A state championship game, against North Tama. Before the game, I threw batting practice in one of the cages and didn't move out of the way fast enough. A line drive smacked me right in the chest.

Great, I thought, gasping for breath. I'm going to be in the emergency room when the game begins.

But I recovered, only to nearly lose my breath again watching Norway pull out a 2-1 nail-biter to win the title. I jumped up to run onto the field and join the players. Jim held his hand in front of me.

"They earned this," he said. "Let them celebrate."

I'll never forget that. He was telling me: This isn't about us, it's about them. It's a philosophy I wish more coaches shared.

We waited by the dugout and congratulated each player as he returned.

When I was a boy, reading about state champion teams in the Register, I always wondered what it would be like to know that you were the best. This was the first time I'd ever been part of a championship team, and the wait had been worth it.

What was it like?

Absolutely glorious.

•

The Norway firetruck met the team bus on the edge of town and escorted us to a ceremony at the baseball field. Norway had won its 19th state title, the 12th championship under Van Scoyoc.

It was the last Norway game he ever coached.

There had been some talk that fall about Norway merging with a larger school district, but I was too busy to pay much attention. Jim was worried about it – I knew that – but watching that postgame celebration after the state title game, seeing how happy everybody in town was, I just didn't imagine that anything would ever change.

Leaving Norway after that game was tough. This had been the greatest summer of my life – more fun than playing – and I wanted it to last forever. What was I going to do now to replace it? There were no guarantees I'd be back in Norway the next summer.

It felt as if there were a hole in my heart. Driving home, I had tears in my eyes.

What now?

11
Inheriting a Diamond

I didn't have time to feel sorry for myself.

Norway won its state baseball championship in early August of 1990. My Belle Plaine volleyball team would begin practices in less than two weeks.

It was good for me to get back quickly into coaching. I was the head coach, not an assistant, and the responsibility for my volleyball team's success fell on my shoulders.

But I'll be honest: It was hard at first. Those few months in Norway had rekindled my lifelong love of baseball. It now felt as if my summerlong fantasy camp had ended. I found myself daydreaming a lot that fall about Norway.

But I never could have guessed what would happen next. My imagination isn't that creative.

•

Jim Van Scoyoc called me sometime that fall. The Norway school board had decided to merge the district with a larger one, Benton Community of Van Horne. He had accepted a coaching job with the Detroit Tigers organization. He didn't really have a choice: Benton Community didn't offer him a teaching position.

"I want you to be Norway's coach in its final season," he told me.

I was surprised, but not shocked, by the merger. As I said before, I had heard rumors that summer that it could happen, and as an educator I knew the state was putting great pressure on smaller districts to consolidate with larger ones. It wasn't anything new; it had been going on in Iowa for decades.

But I simply couldn't imagine that Jim wouldn't be coaching the Norway baseball team. I suppose it was the same feeling Green Bay Packers fans had when Vince Lombardi left to coach the Washington Redskins.

Was he sure? I asked.

Yes.

Jim and I trusted each other. When you first meet him, he can be intimidating, almost as if he has constructed a wall around himself to keep others at a safe distance. But I understood it was self-protection. When you're a coach, people approach you with various motives, such as wanting to get their children more playing time. Friends aren't always what you think they are. You become wary.

But Jim confided in me during our summer together. I knew the proposed merger not only angered him, it also saddened him. The town had built something important, and wonderful, over many decades. When people in Iowa heard Norway mentioned, they immediately thought: championship baseball. When people heard Benton Community of Van Horne mentioned, I'm not sure what came to mind.

Jim thought Norway should have fought harder to remain independent. The baseball team had always taken on all comers, no matter what size the school. In Jim's view, school officials should have exhibited some of that same moxie and resolve against state regulators.

He fought hard, but he had lost, and now he was leaving. That prospect made me so sad I probably didn't clearly comprehend the full implication of his phone call.

Wait: He wanted me to replace him?

●

Yes.

Of course.

If that's what you want, Jim, I'll do it.

I'll apply to be Norway's head coach.

Now that several years have passed, I'm still somewhat amazed at how quickly I agreed to do it.

My first instinct, I think, was to please Jim Van Scoyoc. If he thought I was worthy to protect his legacy, then who was I to argue?

I knew baseball. I knew how to coach. I knew the Norway boys, and they knew me. I respected what Norway represented, and I'd guard it like a precious heirloom.

Faith also played a part. From the time I was a boy, my parents had taught me to have faith that God was directing my life, and I believed them. This felt like something I was supposed to do.

The Norway administration conducted a statewide search to find Jim's replacement, but I think I was the only applicant. The district was offering a one-summer deal, and not many teacher/coaches were going to uproot their lives for that. If I had any doubt about the temporary nature of the position, the day I received my coaching contract from Norway, I also received another letter, a pink slip, reminding me that the coaching job would vanish at the end of the summer.

If I had been older, or wiser, perhaps I would have paused to contemplate what I was getting into:

I would be Norway High School's baseball coach during its final season.

My team would have one last chance to win a state baseball title, the school's 20th.

I'd be replacing one of the best high school coaches in Iowa history.

Pressure?

It was about to get worse.

•

When practices began in early May, Jim Van Scoyoc was still teaching in Norway, and still taking care of his cherished baseball diamond. He treated that diamond the way a gardener tends his prize-winning orchids. One of his final acts there was to install brand-new foul poles. The boys in his shop class made them.

It helped me tremendously that he was there. He'd still offer batting and pitching tips to any boy who wanted them (they all did), but he also made it clear to the team that I was in charge. Just as he did with his own teams, he was putting me in the best position to succeed.

But not even Jim could keep our star player in town.

Tyson Kimm attended our first practice, but he had notified us that he planned to spend the summer in San Diego, with his father, Bruce, the former Norway star who was a coach with the Padres.

I certainly understood. How could you possibly blame a teenage boy who wanted to be with his father and hang around major-league players for a summer? I almost asked him to take me with him.

But this was a blow. Tyson was one of the best players in the state, a shortstop who had hit .477 the previous season. He also was our best relief pitcher. He was the first reason to feel optimistic about defending the state title. I was disappointed he wasn't going to play on the team, but I certainly felt no animosity toward him. I knew how close I felt to my own father; it must have been incredibly difficult for Tyson to be separated from his dad.

The other boys were disappointed – Tyson was a stud player. I tried to reassure them. We've still got Shawn Moss to pitch, I said, and Jimmy Walter can play shortstop. There's a lot of talent here. We'll be OK.

I wanted to believe it myself, but there was no denying the impact of Tyson's departure. As a practical matter, we weren't as talented as the Norway team that had won the previous summer. We lacked that one, sure-thing Division I player.

Here, again, Jim Van Scoyoc's confidence reassured me. He had seen plenty of star players depart through graduation over the years, and there were always other boys ready to replace them. That was the beauty of the Norway tradition.

Jim said once that he expected players to emerge from the cornfields, like a scene from "Field of Dreams."

"You knew it was going to happen, but you just wondered who it was going to be."

Yeah, I thought, but those boys had Jim Van Scoyoc to lead them.

This year's team would have me.

●

We had two visitors at our first practice.

Sometime that spring, Ken Fuson, a feature writer for The Des Moines Register, called me at home. Like me, he was a baseball fan who had grown up in Iowa and had been enchanted by Norway's success. How would I feel about letting him and a Register photographer (David Peterson, a Pulitzer Prize winner) follow us to document Norway's final season?

As usual, my enthusiasm trumped common sense. It sounded great; Norway deserved all the attention it could get.

Ken and I would become good friends, but I soon wondered whether I should have agreed to this project. The daily presence of a Register reporter and photographer would be a constant reminder to my players that they weren't simply playing a baseball game, they were playing in Norway's final season. It's hard to field a grounder smoothly while carrying the heavy weight of great expectations on your back.

More pressure.

And if we stumbled, or failed not to win a state championship – or, worse, didn't advance to the state tournament?

The entire state would read all about it, and about the young coach – I was 29 then – who was foolish enough to think he could fill in for a legend. I guess I was just young and confident enough not to worry about it.

Besides, the time for fretting was over. Our first game was scheduled for June 3, against Cedar Rapids Kennedy, a 4A school, one of the largest in the state.

Ready or not, our final season was about to begin.

12
WWJD (What Would Jim Do?)

I admit it: I caved.

Jim Van Scoyoc knew how he wanted his players to look, which included mesh-style baseball caps and long stirrups. The boys told me they preferred professional-style caps, and they wanted to wear their stirrups low, which was the trend in that summer of 1991.

I gave in, but not before more soul-searching than the subject probably deserved. What would Jim think? The last thing I wanted was to displease him, or to look as if we were turning our backs on Norway's tradition. To be honest, it felt as though I was sinning against Coach Van Scoyoc, which amused him greatly when I confessed later.

But here's the thing: It was the only time that season the players tested me. They never talked back; they never fought me on anything. If they second-guessed a decision, they kept it among themselves. It never reached my ears.

The people in town were equally supportive. I'm not sure they thought I had the experience to lead Norway to a final state championship, but they seemed to appreciate the difficult position I and the team were in.

I felt my main job was to be a calming influence. There were still plenty of hard feelings in town about the school merger, but I didn't want it to carry over to the field. They were going to have enough to worry about.

"Guys," I told them, "we've got one thing we've got to accomplish. Let's get it done."

●

We began the season rated No. 1 in Class 1A, the smallest of the state's four classifications. Norway's reputation undoubtedly had more to do with that high ranking than any sober analysis of our team's strengths and weaknesses.

Tyson Kimm was gone, leaving an enormous hole. I had five returning starters, which was a solid nucleus, but my catcher, second baseman and No. 3 pitcher were sophomores. My bench included an eighth-grader (he'd be a freshman in the fall). Our pitching was above average, but not deep. We were probably going to have to outscore teams.

What I had was a team full of gamers.

Shawn Moss, my best pitcher and third baseman, had a heart bigger than home plate.

Eric Freese, the center fielder, was the team leader. If somebody needed a kick in the butt, or a pat on the back, I wouldn't have to do it. He would.

Jim Walter was my shortstop and No. 2 pitcher. Jimmy was versatile; I could play him anywhere.

Kyle Schmidt was a great defensive first baseman. He also could drive the ball, but he tended to strike out a lot and get into horrible slumps.

Brad Day was the catcher. He wore a mullet and was a bit of a free spirit. His antics could drive Jim Van Scoyoc crazy. The year before, Jim told me, "You tell him he'd better get his act together, or he'll never play for me." But I knew he could catch, and he handled pitchers extremely well. They trusted him, and so did I.

I expected a lot that season from Brad Groff, my left fielder. He was probably the best athlete on the team – certainly the quickest – with surprising power. He also hated to lose. I recognized his competitive fire from my own high school days. It was important for Brad to not let his emotions get the best of him.

Tim Arp was a quiet, solid player who filled in at third base when Moss pitched, and he also pitched. Jim Schulte was the second baseman, the nicest kid you would ever meet. Scott Hofer was the right fielder and a left-handed starter. He was the class valedictorian and the target of much kidding. He didn't mind.

I had a few bench players, among them Vaughn Schulte, a freshman and one of my favorites. He would do anything to hang out on a baseball field, from carrying the bats to driving the bus had I asked (I didn't). My assistant coach was Cole Daily, who had been a student of mine in Belle Plaine.

I had one primary goal – to advance to Marshalltown, where the final four teams play in the state tournament. Not making it to Marshalltown would be a disaster, an embarrassing failure.

Play ball.

June 3, 1991

Opening night. Cedar Rapids Kennedy vs. Norway. A pouring rain forced us to reschedule the game for the next day. I remember standing outside Norway High School, watching the rain fall, saying, "The gods of baseball have decreed that if Jim Van Scoyoc ain't coaching, Norway ain't playing."

June 4

It was still raining in Norway, but in one of those strange meteorological quirks, it was sunny in Cedar Rapids, 40 miles away. So we moved the game to Kennedy's field.

I can't remember the last time I was that nervous before a baseball game.

We scored four runs in the fifth inning to take a 6-5 lead. We added three more insurance runs, but they countered with three in the final inning. We held on, 9-8. Shawn Moss had a home run, and Jimmy Walter pitched all seven innings.

I survived. We beat a 4A team. It was a great way to start the season.

June 6

We traveled to Benton Community of Van Horne for a doubleheader. This was the school Norway would be merging with the next season, and I could tell my players were eager to send a message. They did. We swept them.

June 7

We lost our first game of the year, 6-3, in our home opener vs. Marion.

When Jim Van Scoyoc put Norway's season together, he scheduled varsity doubleheaders, figuring his teams needed the experience. He told me that some coaches would want to play their junior varsity teams in the second game, but he advised me not to do so.

The Marion coach pulled his starters in the second game. We rolled, 17-3.

June 11

This was a perfect example of how Jim tested his teams. We played a doubleheader against City High of Iowa City, a ranked team in 4A. We won the first game, 9-8, with a four-run rally, then lost the nightcap, 5-4. Two great games. You win one and you lose one.

Norway boys knew they weren't going to get through a regular season undefeated. Not with a schedule filled with larger schools. They hated losing, but they weren't poor sports about it, nor did they get down on themselves. They loved the challenge.

With Tyson Kimm in San Diego, our pitching depth was going to be a problem. If you could throw strikes, you were going to pitch. I had to put two sophomores, Tim Arp and Jim Schulte, into the mix.

June 14

This was a difficult doubleheader for me. We were playing Belle Plaine, the school where I taught. We won both games, 12-2 and 21-1. The second game was ugly, and I felt terrible. I wish Belle Plaine hadn't even been on the schedule. I loved those kids as much as the Norway kids. Belle Plaine played their junior varsity in the second game, and afterward I apologized to their players. They told me not to worry about it, but it wasn't a good feeling.

We won doubleheaders on June 20, 21, and 22, putting our season record at 13-2. My only concern at that point was pitching. The boys' arms were getting tired, and we were giving up more runs than Norway teams normally do.

June 24

I told the team, "This is going to be the test to find out how good we really are." Cedar Rapids Jefferson, the No. 1-rated team in Class 4A, was arriving in Norway for a doubleheader. Jefferson had swept both games the year before.

They had 1,182 students in three grades of high school; we had 104 in four.

"Come on, red caps," I told them. "Let's play Norway baseball."

If the first game was a test, we flunked. Their stud pitcher, Colin Mattiace, who was being watched by major-league scouts, threw a perfect game. We lost, 12-0, in a game called after five innings because of the 10-run rule.

I was nervous. The games had attracted a huge crowd. I tried to remain calm, but if my players looked, they might have seen me spitting sunflower seeds at a machine-gun pace in the dugout.

The second game didn't start any better. Jefferson scored three runs in the first, but Jimmy Walter rediscovered his curveball and settled down after that. We rallied for four runs in the fifth, and they tied the game, 4-4, in the sixth. The game remained tied through the seventh.

Extra innings.

In the bottom of the eighth, Kyle Schmidt struck out. Brad Groff walked, then stole second. Scott Hofer popped up to the pitcher. With two outs, Brad Day singled to center and Groff scooted home with the winning run.

The first game felt as if it had occurred 10 years earlier. The nightcap was a terrific team win, and the boys celebrated in a heap on the field. One thing it proved: These guys weren't ever going to give up. They would give me, and their town, everything they had.

I stayed behind to drag the field, clean the dugouts and turn out the lights. On the way home, I saw the boys reliving the night at one of Norway's three soda pop machines. I honked and they waved back.

We were a team.

It had been a very good night.

13
Showdown

On the morning of July 14, readers of the Des Moines Sunday Register discovered a four-page special section in their newspaper titled, "The Final Season." It described the historic importance of baseball in Norway and our quest for one more state championship.

The idea was to set the stage for state tournament play, which would begin that week. But as I read the story and looked at the photographs, I thought a more accurate headline would have been, "Hey, Kent, You'd Better Win."

There was this quote from former Norway star Mike Boddicker, who was then pitching for the Kansas City Royals: "We played the giants, and we beat them. I think it was instilled in us. We knew we had the best team in the state. We believed that."

And Tyson Kimm added this: "If you don't win the state championship, then you failed. Second is nowhere near to where you're supposed to be. We finished second when I was a sophomore. You just sort of sensed that the town felt let down, and you felt a little guilty."

One of the largest photographs showed me, sitting in the dugout, my chin resting on the end of a bat, looking pensive. It perfectly depicted my feelings that season. It was different the previous year, when I could joke and have fun with the players. There was more distance as a head coach. It was lonely at times.

I was a wreck, not eating or sleeping well. We weren't as good as we were the previous year. Everyone seemed to think that Norway would coast to another title. I knew better. It was never easy. All it takes to knock you out is one stud pitcher throwing the game of his life.

There was another cause for concern. All season long, Burlington Notre Dame and Norway had been trading the top ranking in Class 1A. At that point, they were No. 1. We were No. 2. They were playing a tough schedule, too. They looked dangerous.

And they were on our side of the bracket. To get to Marshalltown, to the final four of our class, we would most likely face them. A showdown loomed.

●

Like a tired racehorse staggering down the homestretch, we were gasping to hit the finish line of the regular season.

We lost Tim Arp to a broken hand not long after the exciting doubleheader with Cedar Rapids Jefferson, which required me to scramble. I had to find someone else to play third base, but also replace him in the pitching rotation.

Anyone with an arm got a chance. Jim Schulte filled in, and I even started catcher Brad Day one game. By the end of June, I had a roster full of tired arms, and the scoreboard reflected it:

Cedar Rapids LaSalle 16, Norway 14.

West Delaware 14, Norway 10.

Norway 22, Vinton 18.

Even Benton Community gained a measure of revenge. They beat us in early July, 19-13.

We were in survival mode, splitting doubleheaders instead of sweeping them, giving up far more runs than Norway teams traditionally do. We got swept in a doubleheader against Cedar Rapids Regis on July 10, one of the low points of the season for me. It was rare when we couldn't take at least one game from the larger schools; the boys would get fired up for them. To get swept was disheartening.

But then we rallied the next night and split a twinbill with Waterloo East, which would go on to win the Class 4A title that year. My boys continued to amaze me with their resiliency.

They weren't afraid to play anybody. Iowa City. Cedar Rapids. Waterloo. The New York Yankees. Bring them on. They weren't cocky about it, but they weren't going to apologize for being on the same field, either. They had a little bit of a chip on their shoulder, as if they represented every tiny school in the state.

All season long, I had tried to act in a way that would have made Jim Van Scoyoc proud. I think I served as a calming effect, which the team, and the town, needed. This was still Jim's team; I told everyone that. I never felt as though I had to put my mark on them. Mostly, I tried to keep the pressure I was feeling away from them. Their job, I told them, was to play ball, not pick sides in the town debate.

We finished the regular season with a record of 25-12. It certainly wasn't Norway's finest regular season, but given the obstacles, I'm not sure anyone could have expected much more out of us.

At one of our last games, umpire Marv Bell pulled me aside after the coaches' meeting at home plate. Marv was to baseball umpiring in Iowa what Jim Van Scoyoc was to coaching.

"Hey, Kent, I just want to tell you one thing," he said. "I'm sure you've heard a lot of people say this isn't your team. I just want you to know you've done a nice job of working with these kids this summer, and you deserve a lot of credit."

He'll never know how much that meant to me. I've never forgotten it.

•

One and done.

Every school in Iowa qualifies for the state tournament. You keep playing until you lose or win the championship. We were seven victories away from the title, one loss away from taking off the Norway uniform forever.

I tried to keep everything simple. There was no rousing pep talk. Just play Norway baseball, I told them. That was my mantra all summer long.

We began well, beating Iowa Mennonite, 6-2, on July 15, then routing Lone Tree, 15-1, two nights later.

Tim Arp returned on July 19, and we outlasted Deep River of Millersburg, 7-4. Shawn Moss struck out the side to end the game.

We played Bellevue Marquette in Lowden on July 23. This would be a test.

The game was tied, 1-1, through four innings, then we scored three in the fifth and another run in the sixth for a 5-1 lead.

But my pitcher, Jim Walter, was tiring. He gave up a leadoff walk in the seventh and final inning. That runner eventually scored, cutting our lead to 5-2.

Then it got interesting. They loaded the bases with two outs. Their first baseman crushed one of Jimmy's pitches down the left-field line, back... back...back.... From where I was sitting, it was a grand slam, and we now trailed, 6-5.

"Foul ball!" the umpire cried.

I exhaled like a just-pardoned condemned man. Jimmy then struck out the kid to end the game.

After the game, left fielder Eric Frese rushed up to me.

"Coach, that ball was fair," he said.

There was no time to savor our good fortune.

That showdown I had predicted a month earlier was now at hand. We'd play Burlington Notre Dame two nights later in Muscatine. No. 1 vs. No. 2. The winner advanced to Marshalltown. The loser's season would be over.

●

My nerves were shot. I think the players might have been anxious, too, because they didn't start out with their customary confidence. We made a costly error in the second inning and quickly fell behind, 3-0.

But Shawn Moss was his normal gutsy self. He was in trouble all night long, scattering 11 hits, but Burlington Notre Dame wouldn't cross home plate again that season.

We tied the score in the third, took the lead in the fifth, and blew it open in the sixth, winning 10-3.

We were headed to Marshalltown.

The long bus ride back to Norway was wonderful. The boys were feeling good about themselves, and I felt a profound measure of relief. I had expected a nail-biter.

I had achieved my biggest goal, getting them to the final four of the state tournament. Anything else would be icing on the cake for me, but not for my players.

Their goal hadn't changed since the first day of practice. It had been their goal the year before, and the year before that. It was the same goal that had been passed from one generation to the next in Norway like a lucky bat:

Win it all.

14
Two Outs, Two Strikes, Nobody On

Beating Burlington Notre Dame calmed me considerably. The next week at practice, the boys seemed to move with a renewed sense of enthusiasm.

You have to understand. For them, Marshalltown, Iowa, the site of the state tournament, was a big city. They asked where we were going to eat before our semifinal game against Twin River of Bode. When I told them the Perkins restaurant, they were excited. I had to get approval from the principal's office.

The instant we loaded the bus to Marshalltown, my jittery nerves made a return appearance, complete with churning stomach. I didn't talk the entire ride. At the restaurant, I might have raked my fork through the omelet once. I tried not to let the players see how nervous I was.

George Funk, the Marshalltown athletic director, greeted us at the baseball field and congratulated me on our season. Walking into the locker room felt like the scene in "Hoosiers," when the Hickory boys get a tour of the gym in which they will be playing.

As the boys stretched, I sat in the dugout and reflected. I said a prayer of thanks, and asked God to let the best team win (of course, I figured God knew we were the best team). When I saw my parents enter the ballpark, I got a little teary-eyed, thinking about all those games of catch in the backyard, and how they had led to this moment.

The other memory that remains vivid was the introduction of the lineups. Hearing the public address announcer say, "And the head coach of the Norway Tigers ... Kent Stock," was even better than what I had imagined as a child: "And the starting second baseman for the St. Louis Cardinals ... Kent Stock."

I had nothing to worry about. We cruised, 7-0. Shawn Moss tossed a five-hit shutout.

One more to go.

●

After the game, the boys wanted a steak dinner. I told them I didn't have prior approval for that. Besides, I didn't think the team had eaten dinner together after the semifinal game the previous year, and I was still determined to follow Jim Van Scoyoc's game plan (as it turned out, they had, he informed me later).

I could tell the guys were disappointed, so I made them a deal: Win the championship game, and I'll make sure you get steaks.

●

The sound of baseball cleats clicked across the cement floor of the locker room at Marshalltown High School. My players looked and sounded loose, which was always a good sign.

It was almost noon on Aug. 3, 1991. In a few moments we'd take the field for the Class 1A championship game. My parents were in the stands, along with Mel Murken, my high school baseball coach in Ankeny.

Jim Van Scoyoc couldn't be there, but I knew he had been following us.

"You're ready," he had written me. "They're ready."

Jim Walter would be starting for us in the title game. When he was good, he could beat anybody, but I had pitched him a lot that summer and his stamina concerned me. Should he falter, I didn't have a great alternative. Shawn Moss was spent, and my other relievers were average at best.

We would be playing South Clay of Gillett Grove, a school from northwest Iowa. I knew very little about the Spartans. I learned later that their pitcher, Ryan Gross, was scheduled to get married that night, so obviously they had advanced further in the tournament than even they had expected.

We would be favored, but there's nothing more dangerous in sports than Cinderella on a roll. They had nothing to lose. We were the Goliath among Class 1A schools, the baseball power with a truckload of trophies in our case. They were playing with house money, more than enough to buy plenty of slingshots.

In the movie about our season, the character named Kent Stock gathers his players together and leaves them with this: "How do you want to be remembered?"

I didn't use those exact words, but the sentiment was similar. Mostly, I wanted the boys to know how proud I was of them, and how honored I felt to be their coach, win or lose.

"You're playing for everyone who has ever worn a Norway jersey," I told them. "They're with you today. Let's finish this off with a state championship. Let's get this done. Just go out and play your game."

That had always been good enough.

●

Eric Frese grounded out to short.

Shawn Moss grounded out to second.

Jim Walter grounded out to short.

South Clay's pitcher set us down in the first inning on seven pitches.

I wasn't particularly worried. My boys had confidence that, given enough chances, they could solve any pitcher. The perfect game thrown by Cedar Rapids Jefferson's pitcher earlier in the year had been an exception. We scored a lot of runs that season.

In their first, Jimmy Walter gave up a walk, but faced only four hitters.

We went down in order in the second. The Spartans scored two runs in their half.

We finally got a base runner in the third, on a leadoff walk, but Jim Schulte grounded into a double play. Eric Frese then collected our first base hit, a single, but Shawn Moss struck out to end the inning.

We went down in order in the fourth.

We were in a ballgame. The South Clay pitcher, Ryan Gross, was spectacular. It was what I had feared: a young man pitching the game of his life when it mattered most.

In the top of the fifth, we cracked the scoreboard. Brad Day singled and eventually scored on a wild pitch.

We took the lead, 3-2, in the next inning. Brad Groff slugged a home run, and back-to-back singles by Jim Schulte and Tim Arp knocked in Scott Hofer with the go-ahead run.

Norway was six outs away from capturing its 20th and final state championship. A lesser opponent might have been intimidated by all that tradition and folded.

South Clay was not that kind of team.

And Jimmy Walter was running out of gas.

●

Here's how South Clay's sixth inning began:

Single.

Error.

Wild pitch.

Sacrifice fly, scoring the tying run.

Single, scoring the go-ahead run.

Another wild pitch.

Walk.

Walk.

The bases were loaded with one out. Jimmy Walter had been a warrior, but he had nothing left. I walked onto the field and pointed to third base.

"Shawn," I said.

All season long, whenever I needed an out or a big play, I called on Shawn Moss. He wasn't the best athlete on the team, but he was the fiercest competitor. He was my Bob Gibson.

But this was probably too much to ask. He had just pitched seven innings two days earlier.

"Keep us in it," I pleaded.

He struck out the first batter he faced. Two outs.

The next batter flied out to second.

We were down by a run with three outs to go.

•

Ryan Gross showed no sign of weakening. Now that he had regained the lead, the South Clay pitcher seemed determined to display the state championship trophy at his wedding reception later that evening.

Shawn Moss grounded out to third.

Jim Walter flew out to center.

Two outs and nobody on.

I paced the third-base box. There was no strategy to impart. This was pure baseball, pitcher vs. hitter. You were either good enough to hit the ball, or you weren't.

"Come on, Kyle," I said, clapping my hands. "Get something started."

What would I tell them? In the back of my mind, I was already rehearsing. My players were going to feel as if they had let down their entire town. It was the sort of disappointment that could shadow and haunt them the rest of their lives. They had played too hard to deserve that.

Over the course of his high school career, Kyle Schmidt had come to the plate 13 times in state tournament games at Marshalltown. He was 0-for-13.

Two strikes.

I clapped my hands.

"You can do it," I said.

Kyle was a soft-spoken young man, one of the most popular players on the team. His father, Francis, was a high school janitor who occasionally drove our team bus. He was one of our biggest fans.

I can imagine how Jack Buck might have called the next pitch:

"Three balls, two strikes, nobody on, two out. The Norway Tigers trail South Clay by a run. Norway's chance to win their final game in their final season is

on the line. This is the ballgame, folks. Kyle Schmidt digs in, Ryan Gross gets his sign. Here comes the pitch ... and he SWINGS...."

Kyle crushed the ball. When it left his bat, I thought he had tied the game with a home run. Instead, it bounced against the center-field fence, and Kyle lumbered into second with a stand-up double.

We had life, but nothing had changed. We were still down by a run, still in desperate need of yet another big hit.

Brad Groff was next. He had homered the previous inning, but now he was behind in the count.

One ball, two strikes, two outs. The tying run at second.

Another pitch, another swing, and another smoking double.

Norway 4, South Clay 4.

•

Brad Day grounded out to end the inning, but a sense of peace swept over me. I knew we were going to win. The Spartans, as valiant as they were, had missed their opportunity. You don't give Norway another chance.

My serenity didn't last very long.

Shawn Moss recorded two quick outs in the bottom of the seventh, but back-to-back singles and a walk loaded the bases once again for South Clay. Shawn was pitching on fumes, but he was still my best option. Any number of things – a walk, a balk, an error, a passed ball, a wild pitch, a hit batter – would hand South Clay the victory.

Shawn wasn't finished. A ground ball to second ended the threat and sent us into extra innings.

In the eighth, Jim Schulte singled and Tim Arp reached on an error. Shawn – did I mention how clutch he was? – knocked in two runs with a double, and we scored another run on an error.

Shawn struck out the first two batters in the bottom of the eighth. In our final three games of the year, Shawn had given up only three runs in 16⅔ innings, and none since the second inning of our substate game against Burlington Notre Dame.

A grounder to second ended the game.

Norway 7, South Clay 4.

I have witnessed my two daughters being born, so I know there is a joy greater than winning a state championship baseball game.

But, boy, it's right up there.

The next morning, in the Register, Ken Fuson's story ran on the top of the front page:

"Incredibly, amazingly, miraculously, Norway High School won its final baseball game."

•

Just as Jim Van Scoyoc had done the previous year, I remained in the dugout while the guys celebrated on the field. This was their moment.

When a television crew reached me, the first thing I did was thank Jim for the opportunity to coach his team.

But I didn't notice what was happening on the field. After that final out, as the boys whooped and hollered, an adult walked out to the field and escorted Kyle Schmidt away from the pile. It was his uncle, and he had distressing news.

While we were rallying to win the game, Kyle's father had suffered a heart attack in the parking lot. He had been taken by ambulance to the Marshalltown hospital.

As word spread, our celebration quickly grew muted. The players didn't know what to do, so they quickly gathered their belongings and left the field. They were worried about their friend's dad. Francis was like part of the team, as the team bus driver, and as a vocal supporter. During the ups and downs of the season, he would always offer me words of encouragement.

In the eerie quiet of that victorious locker room, I spotted Ken Fuson and shook my head.

"Do you believe this life?"

15
Down to Earth

_____

We showered, dressed and left the Marshalltown baseball complex. At a restaurant in town, the conversations were subdued. We had heard that Francis Schmidt was still alive, but we didn't know his prognosis. For all we knew, he could have been fighting for his life at that very moment.

Leave it to Kyle to save the moment, just as he had in the championship game.

He joined us in the restaurant.

"They think he's going to be OK."

The news had the same effect as pulling the cork on a shaken champagne bottle. It was the first time since the final out that the boys could exhibit any unrestrained emotion, and the rest of the meal was filled with much laughter and good cheer. The boys could enjoy their well-earned steaks.

When I think back to that season, I'll never forget Kyle's clutch hit, of course, or Shawn Moss's undaunted courage. But the scene that I most enjoy returning to occurred in that restaurant. The mood was a combination of joy, pride and, yes, relief. It was just us, this band of baseball brothers, who had accomplished one of the hardest things in sports, winning when everyone expected it.

How did they want to be remembered?

They proved it on the field – as champions.

●

Unlike the year before, the Norway firetruck did not meet us at the edge of town. We gathered at the baseball field, but it was a much more restrained scene than the previous season.

Last year, a large group had gathered. This year, it was mostly the parents of team members.

I'm guessing that for many people in town, the bitter fight over the fate of the high school had drained them. Seeing the team for the final time was either too painful, or they had already moved on.

As we got off the bus, somebody was there to collect the jerseys from the boys. Another team in town would be using them, and they wanted to make sure our players didn't leave with them.

That ticked me off. The timing was terrible. These boys had just played their hearts out, and now the priority was to grab their jerseys, still stained with dirt and sweat from the title game? Bad form.

Some of the boys left with their jerseys anyway. That was fine with me. I might have taken mine home, too. Can't remember, your honor.

The tempered town reaction was a fitting reminder that the final season was indeed over, for the team, the town, and for me.

It had been a dream come true, but reality beckoned once again.

•

During the baseball season, I had received calls from the parent of a baseball player at City High in Iowa City who was dissatisfied with the current baseball coach. Would I be interested in replacing him?

First of all, I said, I wasn't interested in taking somebody's job. I certainly wouldn't have appreciated it had a parent plotted behind my back. I thanked her for the interest, but committed to nothing.

But the truth was, that would have been a great position. City High was a 4A school, a traditional sports powerhouse, and I thought about the juggernaut that could be produced if you merged Norway fundamentals with City High's stable of athletes.

When the season ended, the City High baseball coach resigned, and I applied to replace him. Looking back, I think that parent probably hurt me. She undoubtedly lobbied for me, and I'll always wonder whether that irritated the athletic director. Maybe he mistakenly thought I had been conspiring behind the scenes. Who knows?

What I do know is, I didn't even merit an interview.

"It takes a pretty keen person to break into the Iowa City school district," the letter said, "and at this time we've offered the job to somebody else. Thank you for applying."

I guess I just wasn't keen enough.

It worked out for the best. You're always in the spotlight as a high school coach, and the light shines much brighter, even harshly, at the largest schools. It showed me what Class 4A athletics were all about. Most of the pressure and stress occurred off the field. Such schools had no patience for rebuilding years.

My experience with Iowa City had soured me to the point where I didn't apply for any other baseball coaching jobs. And nobody beat down my door to hire me, either.

Maybe they considered me a one-hit wonder, just a fluke who had inherited a championship team and had gone along for the ride.

Whatever. I always said it was still Jim Van Scoyoc's team, but I do believe I made a difference that season. I kept the players together when people in town were angry and divided. Having been there before, I wasn't trying to shove 50 new concepts down their throats. I'd like to think I shouldered the extra pressure so the boys could focus on baseball. I'm not trying to overdramatize my role, but I don't feel compelled to disparage it, either.

I had resigned myself to the idea that I might never coach baseball again, but the mourning period was brief.

Volleyball season in Belle Plaine was starting again.

●

When school started that fall in Belle Plaine, I had two new titles: junior high building head and athletic director.

My duties essentially were the same as those of a junior high principal, but I lacked the master's degree needed for that title.

Watching my father, I'm sure, influenced my decision to become a teacher. Dad never brought work home with him, and he seemed satisfied with his career. He was the model of someone who loved his job.

My first year in Belle Plaine, I taught seven classes in an eight-period day. I felt comfortable in front of a class, which I attribute to Carl Troxel's public speaking class at Ankeny High School.

The first four years, I was a full-time high school business teacher. The next three years, I divided my time between high school and junior high.

I discovered that I really enjoyed the younger students. They could still be molded. If you had to discipline a junior high student, he might still like you the next day. If you disciplined a high school student, he tended to hate you forever. Or at least until he graduated.

The longer I taught, the more I felt the walls closing in on me. You spend all day in the same room, rotating in a new group of 25 students every 45 minutes. It was becoming monotonous, and I needed a new challenge.

When the junior high building head was promoted to high school principal, I applied for his job and got it. I would be in charge of the junior high building and all K-12 activities, like athletic events. I'd also teach three social studies classes.

It was a full plate, but I welcomed the change.

●

That October, I received a phone call at home.

The person identified himself as Tony Wilson, a video producer from Des Moines. He had read the *Register's* coverage of the Norway baseball team and thought the story would make a great movie. Would I object if he pursued the idea?

I checked the calendar. No, it wasn't April Fools' Day, but I remained confident that somebody was playing a prank. Maybe my brother was getting back at me for all those times I knocked him down on the basketball court.

I can't remember whether I actually hung up on Tony – I'm generally more polite than that – but I laughed and ended the conversation as quickly as possible.

A movie, eh?

Good one.

16
A Full Plate

Tony Wilson called back.

He was serious about the movie. Would I meet him and his partner for dinner?

Sounded interesting. Sure.

Tony and his partner, Mike Mars, arrived in a Mercedes-Benz. I sat in the back, on those plush leather seats, and thought: These guys must be serious. We then had dinner at Flannigan's restaurant, one of the nicer places in the Iowa City area. I was impressed.

They asked dozens of questions, about Norway, the final season and my role. Mike seemed to be the more aggressive of the two, a go-getter type. Tony was hard to read. He was thin with curly hair, soft-spoken, and he could sometimes come across as aloof. He asked great, probing questions, but I couldn't really tell what he was thinking. He'd be a great poker player.

As I got to know him better over the years, I realized that Tony's personality reflects his creative mind. He's usually preoccupied with his current project, and what he needs to do next to make it come alive.

He thought the Norway story had a lot of potential. Small schools were falling by the wayside, as the pressure to consolidate mounted. That may have made the most sense economically, but there was a cost, too. The state and the country could be forfeiting values that were worth keeping – like hard work, never giving up, never backing down to a bigger foe. Wasn't that what Norway baseball had stood for all those years?

To me, it sounded wonderful, but preposterous. The odds of a video producer from Des Moines selling a movie to Hollywood seemed even greater to me than the odds that Norway could rally with two outs and two strikes in the state championship game.

But I could tell they had done their homework, and they were passionate about the subject. When they asked whether I would participate, I agreed, on one condition: Jim Van Scoyoc would have to participate as well.

They offered each of us $1,000 for the rights to our story. When I got the contract, I noticed that Jim hadn't signed it yet, so I put an asterisk after my signature and wrote, "Contingent upon Jim Van Scoyoc's signature." He eventually signed, too.

It was a two-year contract. I don't think Jim or I ever expected to hear from them again.

●

The new duties in Belle Plaine kept me running, but I enjoyed the freedom of not being tied to a classroom.

I was responsible for disciplining students, and I quickly discovered the importance of having the support of parents. In a small community like Belle Plaine, the word of a teacher or a school administrator is golden. It's different in larger school districts, I would discover later.

The demands of being the school district's activities director were relentless. There were games to schedule, referees to hire, contracts to sign.

It seemed as though I was attending another game every night of the week. Thank goodness for my secretary, Mitch Robinson. I would have been overwhelmed without her.

It was a juggling act. Say, for an example, that a student had been kicked out of class and told to see me. If I were teaching my social studies class, the child would have to sit outside my room and wait for the class to end. And on the way to my office, we'd probably have to check in with Mitch to make sure we had referees for that night's junior varsity football game. By the time I finally talked with the misbehaving youngster, he had probably forgotten what he did to get into trouble in the first place.

I certainly didn't need any more duties, but that's what I got.

In 1993, the high school baseball coach resigned, and the expectation was that I would replace him. After all, I was the whiz kid who had coached Norway to a state championship. Who better to lead Belle Plaine to glory?

I knew it was a mistake. Belle Plaine did not have the baseball tradition or history that Norway did; Belle Plaine boys grew up dreaming of winning a state wrestling title, not hitting a game-winning grand slam. Baseball was an afterthought, just something to do before wrestling practices began.

Turning a program around takes time. I knew that from my work with the volleyball team. We were routinely included among the top 10 schools in our class when the state's volleyball rankings were released, but that was accomplished when I was teaching. Now I had so many other demands, I knew it would be almost impossible to devote enough time to rebuild the baseball program.

I accepted the job anyway, of course. Part of it is my personality; trying to please people is in my DNA. Part of it was wanting to get back out on a baseball field. I had missed it.

I coached baseball in Belle Plaine for three years, and I'm not sure we ever finished above .500. It undoubtedly would have been less frustrating had I not spent those two championship summers in Norway. I thought I could take the experience gained there and transfer it to Belle Plaine. Had I stayed another 10 years, I might have been able to do so.

●

One day at school, Mitch Robinson told me I had a phone call. Someone named Tony Wilson was on the line.

It was 1994, two years after I had signed the movie contract. To be honest, I don't think I ever thought of it again.

Tony offered an update on what he had been doing. He was part of a group opening a new business called Applied Art and Technology in Des Moines, which had kept him busy. But he was still interested in the Norway movie.

He wanted to extend our contract – for $1. What the heck. I agreed.

And this would be our arrangement over much of the next decade. Tony would call every so often, telling me he was still interested, reporting on the progress that was being made, and I would return to my normal life, thinking that I'd believe a movie was going to be made when I saw it.

It was fun to joke with friends that I had a big movie deal lined up, but my expectations could not have been lower. Tony Wilson was an earnest, well-meaning guy, but come on. The middle of Iowa is a long way from Hollywood.

●

My stomach was churning again.

I knew this feeling. It reminded me of sitting in the dugout, waiting for Norway to play the state title game in 1991.

But this was October 1995, and I was standing in the Belle Plaine High School gymnasium, waiting for my volleyball team to play Grandview Park Baptist in a best-of-five match. This was the substate finals; the winner would advance to the state tournament in Cedar Rapids.

This was a great time to be in Belle Plaine. For the first time in school history, the football team had qualified for the state playoffs, and my great friend Reece Dodd was the head coach. He'd gone for a two-point conversion to win a game two nights earlier, but Belle Plaine was stopped short. The referee's decision was controversial. From where I stood, we had crossed the goal line, but it was a great game, and I was proud to be part of it as the athletic director.

Now it was our turn. We had won seven conference volleyball titles during my 12 years as head coach, but we had not gotten over the hump and advanced to the state tournament. This would be our chance to make school history, too.

But I forgot to mention something: Grandview Park Baptist, a Des Moines school, was the top-ranked team in our class.

I knew we had a chance. My 1995 team had three all-state players: Tara Walton, Tamara Ewoldt and Desiree Beal. Amy Wagner and Amber Friedman, the setters, were my coaches on the floor. Erin Eckel was a 6-foot middle hitter who hadn't played much her junior year. Now a senior, Erin had developed into a fine middle blocker. She was yet another example of a young person who could have quit, but persevered and flourished. Sarah DeMeulenaere worked the back row, digging every spike that rocketed her way.

This was the program that I had built. These were players whom I had coached. So when I tell you that we upset No. 1 Grandview Park Baptist, three games to two, I felt a satisfaction even greater than when Norway won the state baseball title.

In the state tournament, we beat Underwood in the first round, then lost to Treynor, 3-1, in the semifinals. It was a good match. A couple of breaks and we might have won, but nobody was going to beat Eldora-New Providence for the title that year. They had a player, Abbie Brown, who was phenomenal.

There is no third-place consolation game in volleyball, so we had to be satisfied with finishing in the top four. I couldn't have asked those girls for anything more. Success is determined by getting the most out of your abilities, not necessarily the final score. Those players got the most of their abilities, and then some.

Many years later, during a childbirth class, when the men were asked whether they wanted a son or a daughter, I was the only future father who said I wanted a daughter. I hope the girls on that 1995 team, and all my volleyball players, understand that I was thinking of them when I answered that question.

That year was an affirmation for me. I wasn't a one-season or one-sport fluke. I had taken two different teams from two different towns in two different sports to state tournaments. A boys' team and a girls' team. I had proven to myself that I could coach.

Coaching volleyball was a welcome diversion, because my personal life was in disarray. I had been married in December 1990 – the winter before I took over the Norway baseball team – and five years later it was clear that a divorce was inevitable.

In the worst times of my life, I could always hear the voice of my parents, telling me that God had a plan for me and I should trust Him. Everything would work out the way it was supposed to work out.

I'll admit it, my patience was sorely tested during those days. But when the 1996-97 school year began, I quickly discovered, once again, that my parents had been right.

17
Meant to Be

———

The ruse I presented to Laurie Gaddis over Christmas break in January 1997 will not land me in the Dating Strategies Hall of Fame. But I would just like to point out that it worked.

"Say, Laurie," I said. "I got a couple of shirts for Christmas that I need to return to Von Maur in Cedar Rapids. Since I'm going to be in town anyway, would you like to go out for dinner?"

OK, there weren't any shirts, a white lie that Laurie forgave me for later, long after we had enjoyed a wonderful dinner that night at The Sand Trap restaurant in Cedar Rapids.

It's appropriate that clothes figured into our first date, because her first memory of me was that I was wearing blue-and-white-striped shorts and a plaid Polo shirt while leading my first faculty meeting, in August 1996, before the Belle Plaine school year had begun. She thought, "There's no way that man's married. No one would let him out of the house that way." In my defense, I'll say only that the school's air conditioning wasn't working, and I'm color-blind. And while I don't think I've ever owned a plaid Polo shirt, I won't argue with her memory.

I didn't know a great deal about Laurie during that first faculty meeting.

I knew that she had been hired to teach in the district's talented and gifted program, and that she previously had been teaching in Texas.

Now, when Laurie and I replay the circumstances that brought us together, we can only shake our heads and say it was meant to be. We say that a lot.

•

Laurie grew up with three sisters in Solon, a town near Iowa City. Her father, Don, whom everyone calls "Butch," and mother, Karen, formed a successful company called CEI "Pacer", where they manufacture truck bodies and semi trailers that are used to carry bulk feed from feed mills to farms.

From the time she was a little girl, Laurie knew she wanted to be a teacher. She loved visiting the classroom of her grandmother, Dorothy Ellingson, who taught youngsters in Cedar Rapids. At night, Laurie would line up her dolls and stuffed animals and pretend to teach them.

After graduating from Solon High School in 1981, Laurie spent two years at Wartburg College in Waverly, Iowa, majoring in music and Spanish. She's an accomplished pianist, and her goal was to teach music, but Waverly is a magnet for talented musicians.

"The competition was fierce," she says. "I practiced all the time, yet the other students seemed to be as good without working all that hard. I thought, 'Maybe I don't have the talent I thought I had.'"

After two years at Wartburg, she transferred to the University of Northern Iowa, where she obtained her education degree in 1986.

That was a tough year to break into teaching, but Laurie got lucky. For some reason, the school district in the border town of McAllen, Texas, loved Iowa-trained teachers. When McAllen representatives discovered on a recruiting trip to UNI's annual teachers fair that she had a minor in Spanish, they nearly offered her a job on the spot.

This is when McAllen got lucky. Laurie's great-aunt and great-uncle lived there, and her grandparents, the Ellingsons, spent winters there, so Laurie was familiar with the city. She accepted the job, figuring that she had endured her last Iowa snowstorm.

She met a man there and was married in 1990, the same year I was.

Laurie eventually obtained her master's degree, in gifted education. She had expected to finish her career there, much the same way I thought I would remain in Belle Plaine, but her marriage ended about the same time mine did.

Her heart broken, she returned to Iowa, to her parents' home.

"My next man was a horse," she jokes, referring to Skip, the pleasure horse she kept at her parents' place.

In fact, she had been in the barn, feeding Skip, in the summer of 1996 when she was told that the elementary principal from Belle Plaine was on the phone. They were looking for someone to teach talented and gifted students in kindergarten through 12th grade, and had heard about her through the UNI placement office. Would she apply?

Laurie hadn't expected to return to teaching right away. She had to look on a map to see where Belle Plaine was. She surprised herself by agreeing to the interview, then surprised herself even more by agreeing to take the job. She would start in the fall of 1996.

It was meant to be.

•

My first impression: Laurie had an excitement about her that glowed. You could tell she loved to teach just by watching her. She wasn't difficult to look at, either, but I tried to keep my early assessments professional.

I didn't see her all that much at school. I was in the junior high building, and she spent all but one hour a day with the elementary students.

It was at the staff Christmas party that year that I discovered how much fun she was. As beautiful as she was, her personality was even more winning. I had been set up on some blind dates, but they weren't half as fun or interesting as Laurie was.

Her first impression: "I always enjoyed talking to him. The staff loved him, the families loved him, the kids loved him. I never heard a student complain about him. I think it's because he was fair. Firm, but fair."

Laurie wasn't exactly sure what to think when I invited her to dinner on my "shirt-exchanging" mission to Cedar Rapids. "I was kind of like, 'Is this a date?'" she says now. "I had my suspicions."

The dinner occurred on Jan. 3. 1997. Have I mentioned that the number 3 is my favorite number? It was my uniform number at Waldorf.

I was more nervous before that dinner than before any baseball or volleyball game I had ever coached. But as soon as we began talking, those fears disappeared. We had a great time, and learned how much we had in common.

We had been previously married and divorced the same years. Each of us still had hope of finding the right person and enjoying a stable marriage. We both wanted children. We both enjoyed educating young people. I had even taken piano lessons as a youngster, so we had that in common, too.

I was smitten, no doubt about it.

•

The next year was a whirlwind.

I normally had a game to supervise at night, so Laurie would go, too, giving us a chance to be together while looking as if we were doing nothing more than serving as dedicated Belle Plaine staff members.

That summer, we were mostly inseparable.

"We did everything together," Laurie says. "We liked each other's families and each other's friends. My sister had just gotten married, and Kent got along well with her husband. They had a boat, and we'd go out on the Coralville Reservoir. We went to festivals and played golf, just had a ball. That's when we realized maybe we could give this marriage thing another shot. I knew I wanted children. I knew I wanted to find a good husband. I knew I wanted another chance."

At one point that summer, we visited Laurie's grandparents, Herb and Dorothy Ellingson, in Cedar Rapids. It turned out that Herb was a huge baseball fan. He said he had grown up in a small town called Norway, Iowa, which was known for its baseball. Maybe I had heard of it.

I know – I wouldn't believe it, either, but it was absolutely true. Laurie's grandfather was from Norway. See what I mean when I say this was meant to be?

I explained my connection to Norway, and about the two years I had spent as an assistant and head coach. Herb knew about the final season, but he didn't realize that I was the person who had taken over the team.

Laurie seemed slightly stunned by this development as well. I hadn't really talked about Norway much. I think she was even more surprised when I told her there was some talk that a movie would be made about that season. But it probably wouldn't happen.

•

I raised the subject of marriage first. I told Laurie that she would not see me proposing on bended knee. When the time was right, we'd just know it.

There was a catch (isn't there always?). During her first year in Belle Plaine, Laurie had been offered, and had accepted, a job teaching talented and gifted students in second through fifth grade in Cedar Rapids. That was a dream job for her.

If we got married, I would commute from Cedar Rapids to Belle Plaine. It was a long drive, but I didn't want to risk losing her.

If we got married ... that seemed to be a recurring subject as the 1997-98 school year began, with me back in Belle Plaine and Laurie beginning her new job in Cedar Rapids.

We looked at the calendar: Jan. 3, 1998, the one-year anniversary of our first date, was on a Saturday, and, as I said, I was always partial to the number 3.

We were married at Westminster Presbyterian Church in Cedar Rapids, the same place Laurie's grandparents had been married. It was a small, intimate gathering, with about 40 family members and a couple of friends.

My mom has described my dad as an answer to a prayer, and that's how I've always regarded Laurie. Best teammate I've ever had. In the game of life, I hit a home run.

18
Change of Scenery

After we were married, Laurie and I lived in the condo in Cedar Rapids that she had bought a year earlier, and I commuted the 40 miles to and from Belle Plaine.

It wasn't an ideal situation, but those long drives provided me the time and isolation to reflect on where I was in life, and more important, where I wanted to go.

I had begun taking classes at Drake University in Des Moines, in a fast-track program to earn a master's degree in administration. I'd need that to reach my ultimate goal of becoming a building principal. Basically, I had all the duties and responsibilities of a junior high principal in Belle Plaine, but not the title or salary.

I loved Belle Plaine. That town had given me my first teaching job, and the people there were enormously supportive. Nobody blinked when I asked to coach the Norway baseball team during those two summers. A part of me will always be a Belle Plainer, as they call themselves.

Even so, my opportunities for advancement there were limited, and I was running myself ragged as a teacher, administrator and athletic director. Don't misunderstand – I wanted those jobs, and I'll always be grateful they were offered to me. But if I was going to be the kind of husband and father I wanted to be, I needed to be home at night more than I was going to be in Belle Plaine.

In the spring of 1998, I tested the market. I interviewed with the Linn-Mar school district in Marion, and Marc McCoy, the junior high principal, offered me the job as his assistant principal. The salary increase would be large enough to cover the cost of my getting a master's degree. It was perfect.

One of the most difficult things I've ever done was notifying the school officials and my friends in Belle Plaine that I was leaving. Laurie still worries that people there blame her for my decision. They shouldn't; I needed a new challenge and a change of scenery. Belle Plaine had been my home for 13 years, but it was time to leave. The timing was right for another reason.

Laurie was pregnant.

●

That was a surprise. I don't think either one of us thought we'd be starting a family quite that quickly, but we were excited by the prospect.

With a baby, the condo in Cedar Rapids would be too small, so we bought a home about eight miles away in the Linn-Mar school district. It's always good to live in the school district in which you're working, and I liked the idea of having my wife and child nearby.

For a long time, I never thought I'd have the chance to be a father. Now here I was, at the age of 36, about to become one for the first time. I couldn't wait.

When my new job started, in the fall of 1998, I quickly realized I wasn't in Belle Plaine anymore. The most obvious difference was the size of the school district. In Belle Plaine, I supervised about 100 students. My first year at Linn-Mar, there were 750 students in seventh and eighth grades. The next year, when the building became a middle school, grades six through eight, we had more than 1,000 youngsters.

There were other adjustments. For the first time in my education career, I wasn't teaching or coaching.

My second year there, I added the title of activities director for the middle school. I was back in the world of athletics, which I loved, but the games were over by 6 p.m., which allowed me to spend nights at home.

I can't say I missed coaching, at least at first, simply because I had so much else to keep me busy. As the assistant principal, I was in charge of discipline, and my decisions were being questioned much more by parents in Linn-Mar than they were in Belle Plaine. It happened often enough to keep me on my toes.

Whatever notions I had about effective parenting were about to be tested in my own home.

●

It was about 9 p.m. on Oct. 29, 1998, when Laurie told me we needed to go to the hospital. She thought it was time.

A false alarm. The nurses reassured us that it happens all the time. Go back home and be patient, they said. When it's really time, you'll know.

How right they were. About 2 a.m., Laurie woke me up.

"This is it!" she said. "It's labor!"

Back we went, to St. Luke's Hospital in Cedar Rapids. We did the breathing exercises we had learned in childbirth classes, but nothing was happening. As the hours of labor continued, Laurie finally consented to some pain medication; she had hoped to endure the birth without it. Still, no baby.

I don't know how much time passed, but Laurie's obstetrician, Dr. Joy

Olson, finally issued her verdict: This wasn't working. It was time to perform a caesarean section.

Laurie pleaded with her.

"Just give me one more hour."

Dr. Olson has the kindest bedside manner I've ever seen, but I had been in enough huddles in my life to see a coach take charge, and that's exactly what she did. The kindly doctor had put on her game face.

"No," she told Laurie, "and here's why."

She listed all the reasons why an emergency c-section was required. Now.

A nurse threw me some scrubs and ordered me to change.

Walking down the hall to the operating room, I was scared to death. I didn't know whom to worry about more – Laurie or the baby. This was certainly not what we had planned.

When I get nervous, I don't freak out, I just get very quiet. That's what I did then, saying a prayer to myself that it would all work out.

The operation went flawlessly.

Kendrie Ann Stock was born at 4:17 p.m. She weighed 9 pounds, 10½ ounces.

During the operation, I remained by Laurie's side, comforting her. The sight of blood still made me pass out. But after Kendrie was born, I faced one of the biggest struggles of my life: Do I stay with Laurie, who had just endured an emergency operation, or do I check on my newborn baby a few feet away? No "Dancing With the Stars" contestant ever moved back and forth as quickly and as often as I did that night.

I was so proud of Laurie, so proud of my daughter, so happy to be a part of it. I know that babies have been born for a good, long time, and I know that I'm not the first father to witness the birth of his child, but when it happens to you, it's magical and magnificent.

•

Laurie remained home on maternity leave with Kendrie through Christmas break that year, then decided to return to school and finish the second semester. After that, we agreed, she would be a stay-at-home mom.

But that left us with a problem: Who would watch our daughter during the semester that Laurie taught?

We began searching for day-care providers, but nothing felt right, a point I casually mentioned to my parents during a visit.

Not long after, I received a phone call from Dad. He had just retired from teaching the previous spring.

"Would you be OK with me coming over and watching her?" he asked. "I'll do your day care. I'd come over on Sunday night and leave on Friday night. It's got to be OK with Laurie, though."

Laurie thought the idea was fantastic.

"Ken is an amazing man," Laurie says about Dad. "Not everyone could have their in-laws live with them. He was a piece of cake. He was so helpful. He did everything for Kendrie that I would have done, and probably did it better than I could have done. Then he'd disappear at night so we could have our own family time. He was just aware of what was needed."

To this day, Kendrie and Dad have a special bond, formed during their six months together. She naturally gravitates to him during family gatherings. It reminds me of the relationship I had with my Grandpa Lee.

•

Life clicked along at a steady pace for the next year or so. Laurie and I grew comfortable in our new roles as parents (and newlyweds). I finished the work on my master's degree, and it felt as if I had finally erased whatever lingering regrets remained from the semester I had been ruled ineligible at Luther College. The new job was a challenge, but a satisfying one.

It was about this time that I heard again from Tony Wilson. He would check in every six months or so, just to let me know he was still working on the movie. I always enjoyed talking to him, but I never allowed myself to get too caught up in his dream. I mean, it had been eight or nine years since Norway's final game. A movie still sounded like "Mission: Impossible."

Only this time, Tony had news to report: He had hired a professional screenwriter, Art D'Alessandro, of Tampa, Fla., who was coming to Iowa to interview me.

We met at a Hy-Vee grocery store in Marion for about three hours. Just as Tony had years earlier, Art wanted to know everything about Norway and my experiences there.

A few months later, I received a copy of Art's script, and I cried. He seemed to have perfectly captured my emotions from that wonderful summer.

Hmm, I thought. Maybe I could allow myself to dream a little.

19
Transitions

Our family grew to four on May 12, 2000, when Kylee Diane Stock was born.

Her birth was not as dramatic as Kendrie's, at least not at first. We knew from the beginning that the delivery would be made by c-section, so we enjoyed a nice dinner the night before.

The problem came after the birth. Laurie's stitches began to burst, and a terrible infection set in. I remember sitting in the hospital room, listening to Dr. Olson argue with another doctor about what they should do. Once again, Dr. Olson took charge, and Laurie recovered.

During a checkup at the doctor's office, one of the nurses said to Laurie, "You're the one we almost lost." I don't think either one of us had realized the true seriousness of her situation.

A year or so later, another health scare would leave all of us shaken.

•

I loved my life: I had a great job, a loving wife, two beautiful daughters, and the dream that a movie about my two years coaching at Norway might become a reality. Things were rolling in the right direction for me. Then I hit a wall.

Dad casually mentioned that he had noticed a lump in his neck and was having trouble swallowing. The doctors had advised him to have the lump removed, so I drove to Des Moines to be with him.

Seeing my dad in a hospital gown, preparing for the procedure, I realized that he wasn't as invincible or immortal as I had thought. He had always been my rock.

Dad was quiet and nervous, and rightly so. The unknown is always more terrifying than the known, and we'd have to wait to find out what the tests indicated. The wait was terrible.

When Dad called, he said he had some good news and some bad news.

"The bad news is that I have lymphoma."

My heart sank.

"They say it's treatable but not curable. The good news is that it's not hereditary."

Typical Dad. During one of the most traumatic moments in his life, he's concerned about his children.

Dad went through radiation treatments, which appeared to put the cancer in remission. A year later, he informed us that a CT scan showed that the lymphoma had returned.

Six months of chemotherapy followed. One week of therapy, two weeks off. He felt terrible. It really beat him down. I remember one Christmas that we couldn't get together because one of our girls was sick and he couldn't risk being around her. It killed me to know what he was going through and not be there to help him.

Once again, the cancer went into remission. I can always tell when he has a checkup looming, because he gets very quiet. But it has been seven years, and the cancer has not returned. Every day he remains healthy is a gift from God.

•

The five years I spent as an assistant principal at Linn-Mar were good ones.

I missed coaching girls volleyball, and there was a time when my name was mentioned to replace the varsity coach, who was leaving. I might have done it, but the superintendent said he didn't really want his principals and assistants coaching sports. I was OK with it. Being able to go home at night was a blessing.

We endured some very emotional moments during my years as an assistant, but I went home at night knowing the buck didn't stop with me. It stopped with Marc McCoy, the principal.

That was about to change.

In the spring of 2003, Linn-Mar Superintendent Joe Pacha stopped by to see me. This was a surprise; he normally dealt with building principals.

Joe had a problem. Linn-Mar was growing so quickly that a new school had been approved, to be called Oak Ridge. Construction had begun, and the K-8 school would be opening that fall.

The woman who had been slated to be the building's principal had taken another job.

"I'd like you to be the Oak Ridge principal," Joe told me, "and I need to know your answer by Monday morning."

This was a Friday afternoon.

Laurie and I discussed it.

"You know what?" I said. "I came to Linn-Mar hoping to be a principal one day. I didn't think it would come this fast, but here it is. This is the way it's supposed to be."

Laurie agreed: "This is what you're here for."

I accepted the job.

•

It was the summer from hell. Everything needed to be done, from hiring teachers to making sure the library had enough books, from overseeing the final stages of building construction to ensuring that the bathroom soap dispensers were filled.

My assistant principal, Dan Ludwig, and I worked nonstop. The driveway entrance wasn't paved until the day before school started, but somehow we managed to open school on schedule. My two proudest moments that year were addressing my first faculty meeting – this was my team now – and watching the students depart on the last day of school. We had survived.

I'm proud of my legacy at Oak Ridge, but I've often said that if someone offered me $200,000 to open a new school, I'd politely decline.

As the principal, you're basically the manager of a small corporation. I had 700 students and about 70 teachers, custodians and other staff members to supervise that first year. I was the police chief, social worker, peacemaker and public face of the institution.

I took everything home with me. I worried about every kid and every adult every day. When I was the assistant principal and a security alarm at school went off, they didn't call me. Now they did, and I'd have to get dressed at 1 in the morning to make sure the building remained standing.

Every day, it felt as if there was a new fire to extinguish. I eventually got settled in the job, but it never became easy, or comfortable.

•

I was certainly too busy during that time to concern myself with the prospects of a Norway baseball movie. Tony would give me updates from time to time, just like always, but there wasn't much to report.

He and Art had been trying to sell the script, but having no success. People were encouraging and offered suggestions, which led to yet another script revision. It became clear that just telling what had happened wouldn't be enough to entice Hollywood. More drama and a love story would be required. There needed to be more to attract young moviegoers.

It struck me that getting a movie made was a little like drilling for oil. You've got to endure a lot of dry wells before a gusher occurs, and it always feels like a miracle when it does.

Somehow, the script reached David Mickey Evans, the director of "Radio Flyer" and "The Sandlot." He liked it, and said he would be interested in directing it.

Then Sean Astin read it. This was the star of "Rudy," the popular Notre Dame football movie, and he had a long resume of impressive movie credits. Sean said he loved the script and was interested in portraying the Kent Stock character.

This was the first time since my initial dinner meeting with Tony Wilson – who, by the way, had borrowed the Mercedes-Benz I was so impressed by that night – that I thought this movie might actually happen.

We had a script. We had a director. We had a star.

Now all we needed was money.

20
Head First

I caught the fever.

It was one thing to have Tony Wilson say he thought the Norway story would make a good movie. It was quite another to have an accomplished director and a movie star say so.

My earlier skepticism evaporated. I now thought this movie was going to happen. I wanted this movie to happen.

Laurie remained wary, but hopeful. As she puts it, "I understood how much it meant to Kent. As I started to understand the uniqueness of Norway, and their success and the history there, I was almost rooting for it to happen. But I'm kind of a skeptic."

I needed to make a decision. At some point, Tony asked me, "Do you want to be a part of this?" What he meant was, "Do you want to take a more active role in making this happen?"

Tony and I were friends, so we could be frank with each other. I truly thought the movie would be a hit. I also thought it would be a great adventure to watch the making of a movie from the inside. How many other Iowa natives get an opportunity like that?

I was back on the diving board. And I jumped, head first.

•

Our goal was to begin filming in 2005, but we first needed to raise $500,000 in development money.

That's what it would take to show the people in Hollywood that we were serious. It would show David Mickey Evans and Sean Astin that we meant business. It would help attract a studio to get involved, which was our primary goal.

Laurie and I invested some money. We asked friends and family members to contribute, and they did. Then it was a matter of thinking of qualified people who might want to invest in the movie, and had the financial resources to do so, and simply asking them.

I agreed to participate in some of the group presentations, and discovered I enjoyed it. Having been a teacher, I was used to standing in front of groups, and I was selling a product I believed in. In fact, the more I talked about the movie, the more excited I became about wanting to see it happen.

Somehow, enough people agreed, and we raised the money. But the Hollywood studios still weren't buying.

I'm not sure what the problem was. Maybe they were interested only in blockbusters. Maybe they wanted Steven Spielberg and Tom Cruise to express an interest. I thought we were offering them a great script and a wonderful movie, but what did I know? This wasn't my world.

It was tremendously frustrating. One day, we'd think that we were about to get picked up by a studio. The next day, it had decided not to participate.

We finally realized that we were not going to begin filming in 2005. In fact, we might not be filming at all.

•

There are two main ways to produce a movie.

You can write a script and have a Hollywood studio buy it. The studio handles the contracts, the filming, the advertising and the distribution.

Or, if that fails, you can produce your movie independently, raising the money yourself to hire the actors and film crews, and then hope it's good enough that a studio will buy and distribute it, or that a distributor will get involved and show your film in theaters.

Having struck out with the studios, we decided in 2005 to go the independent route. It was risky, and would require more money and more investors.

To their credit, David Mickey Evans and Sean Astin could have walked away, but they believed in the movie and stuck with us.

We went to work. In fact, it sometimes felt as if I had a second job.

"That was probably the hardest year of our marriage," Laurie says. "Kent got really involved. He and Tony talked a dozen times a day on the phone. When he wasn't on the phone, he was on the Internet, learning about the movie business. We didn't have him. The movie had him. Friends and family members had invested in this, and that weighed on him a lot."

The problem was, we were always tantalizingly close to a breakthrough. Just one more investor, just a little more money, just one more phone call would put us over the top, we felt. We were constantly scrambling, but it never got to the point where we decided to give up. This was the Norway story, after all. Two outs, two strikes, down by a run ... you don't give up.

It was quite an education. There apparently exists an entire subculture of people in Hollywood who do little else but pretend that they are going to invest in a movie. Folks would commit, then back out when it came time to write a check. I think they just liked posing as big shots, or having people treat them as such.

It was the Iowans who never gave up on the movie, who believed in it, who thought it was a great story that deserved a wider audience. They were the ones who always came through in the clutch. There were times when I thought we were shutting down, and then some miracle would occur and someone else would come through for us. Iowans contributed more than 90 percent of the movie's budget.

I'm still not sure how we did it – dogged work and a lot of begging, mainly – but we raised enough to schedule filming of our movie, called "The Final Season," for the spring and summer of 2006.

●

Our director, David Mickey Evans, was the first to arrive, in April 2006.

A producer showed him the Norway ball field, and the church, and David immediately fell in love with the place. In an eerie coincidence, on the same day that he arrived, funeral services were held for Francis Schmidt, the school janitor who had suffered a heart attack on the day we won the state title. I think at this point, David also thought it was meant to be.

Laurie and I hosted a barbecue for David in our new home in Marion. He wore a black-leather jacket and was incredibly charming, but you could detect the intensity there. One interesting tidbit: He had the logo of several movies he had directed tattooed on his arm. My hope was that "The Final Season" logo would be next. All I could think was, when this guy commits to a project, he really commits.

I met Sean Astin in May. Jim Van Scoyoc and I had been hired to be consultants on the movie, and we were in Cedar Rapids, working with the sports choreographers, who would be designing some of the action sequences. They were working out local athletes who were seeking roles as Norway players and opponents.

As I was hitting ground balls, someone said, "Kent, we need to introduce you to somebody." I turned around, and it was Sean, who got down on his knee and bowed toward me. Then he stood up, grabbed me by the shoulders and said, "You've been in my head for a year."

He had been thinking about me? As I said in that locker room so long ago, do you believe this life?

21
Showtime

Filming began on May 30, 2006, and finished on July 2.

It was a brutal schedule. We worked at least 12 hours a day, often 16, six days a week, taking Mondays off. I had never before worked so hard and had so much fun. Sometimes we'd start at noon and work until midnight, then get up at dawn and do it all over again. Sleep deprivation was a constant companion, but it was hard to fall asleep, even after an arduous day, because there was so much to take in and reflect on.

I had a backstage pass for the making of the movie. Not only that, I also got to relive one of the greatest summers of my life. The superintendent at Linn-Mar, Katie Mulholland, gave me a six-week leave, which I greatly appreciated.

The movie experience reminded me of Norway's run to a state title in one respect – I got to take other people along for the ride. People in Norway and Cedar Rapids could participate in crowd scenes; some even got tiny walk-on roles in the movie. Thousands of people felt a small measure of joy in seeing that movie filmed.

The scope of the production constantly amazed me. It was like this roving factory that roamed from Norway, to Cedar Rapids, and then to other filming locations in northeast Iowa. Anything that appeared on screen – from a background character to a vintage 1980s car – required a written release form. It's stunning how much work is required to produce something that may appear on screen for only a few seconds.

I'm still not sure how David Mickey Evans pulled it off, but I've rarely seen a more focused individual. He knew what he wanted, he didn't have time to waste, and he didn't worry about bruising the feelings of his crew to get it. Then, a half-hour after he'd chewed someone out, he'd be laughing and hugging him. The pressure on David must have been incredible.

One of the best parts about each day was going to David's trailer after filming ended for the day, talking to him about movies, what he had done that day, what he would do tomorrow. It was like auditing a graduate-level course in filmmaking, and I was fascinated, but I didn't envy his lifestyle. A lot was riding on him.

In fact, I think the only person who felt a greater burden was Tony Wilson. Everybody seemed to need something from him – and right now.

We went through so many peaks and valleys. There were so many miracles needed just to get the movie filmed that it always struck me that it was supposed to happen. Call it another one of those meant-to-be moments in my life.

●

People ask me: When did it sink in that the movie was actually happening? I'd have to say it was one day in the production office, when somebody said he wanted to show me something.

In the back room, hanging up, were Norway's red and gray jerseys, which had been perfectly re-created by a uniform company. There was my No. 40, which Sean Astin would be wearing.

Goosebumps.

•

The actors were generous and gracious. I remember thanking Powers Boothe for participating, and he said, "No, Kent, thank you for letting us tell your story." His daughter, Parisse, and son, Preston, also had roles, and the family seemed remarkably close. (Powers and Parisse worked together on HBO's "Deadwood" series.)

Rachael Leigh Cook was delightful, and Michael Angarano was just a super kid. His parents arrived for most of the filming, and you could tell they kept him grounded, even though he might have been one of the biggest stars in the film.

Larry Miller, who portrayed a reporter in the film, was absolutely hilarious. If you don't immediately recognize the name (if you saw him, you'd know), he was the salesman who gave Richard Gere his tie in "Pretty Woman." I think you could produce a pretty decent comedy just by trailing Larry with a camera crew and recording his throwaway lines. His ad libs were as funny as anything in the script.

When we needed comic relief – and given the pressures facing this production, we needed a lot – he supplied it.

Tom Arnold was the one actor who didn't seem all that impressed to be meeting Kent Stock (not that I expected him to be). He sort of politely brushed me aside at first, but he must have been busy, because I later discovered him to be a warm, generous guy. Nobody worked harder to promote the movie, and I've met few people who care as much about Iowa. He has certainly never forgotten his home.

He may not be a movie star, but Mike Boddicker was certainly one of my favorites. Other than Hal Trosky, he's probably the Norway native who enjoyed the most major-league success, pitching for the Orioles, Red Sox, Royals and Brewers, and earning a World Series ring with the Orioles. He worked as a baseball consultant on the movie, and his son, James, snagged a pretty good role. Listening to Mike talk baseball was a daily treat.

Among all the personalities, though, the actor I came to know best was the person who portrayed me, Sean Astin. By the time filming had ended, we had become friends.

●

The first time Sean came to our house, for dinner, I remember thinking, "I can't believe this."

But he immediately put me at ease. He may have come from a Hollywood home – his mother is Patty Duke Astin, after all – and he may have performed in movies since he was a child, but there was no sense of entitlement or arrogance about Sean. In baseball terms, he was a big-leaguer, but he didn't think of himself as superior to a concession stand worker. He would have fit in wonderfully in my neighborhood in Marion.

I'm not suggesting he's ordinary. He's obviously a talented actor; it's impossible to imagine "Rudy" or the "Lord of the Rings" trilogy without him. It's just that he has empathy for, and an innate curiosity about, other people. Perhaps that's why he's so good at portraying them

At that first meeting, Sean and I talked long into the night, about movies, baseball, our careers. He was trying to get to know me for professional reasons, of course, but he also seemed truly interested in the stories about my life.

The next time he visited, on one of his Mondays off, he brought his wife, Christine, and three young daughters with him, and they got along great with Kendrie and Kylee.

We decided to go to the local swimming pool, which I thought was a mistake. Kids would recognize Sean and start swarming him for autographs. Don't worry about it, he said, it won't be a problem.

When we arrived, it happened just as I suspected. Kids started streaming toward us.

"Mr. Stock! Mr. Stock!" they exclaimed, congregating around me.

I'm not sure they even recognized Sean, and he got a big kick out of it. In a small town, he said, the local principal is the celebrity.

During one of our talks, Sean turned serious.

"This movie could change your life," he said. "You're going to have more people in your life than you ever had before, and they're going to want things from you. You've got to think about how to deal with that."

I hadn't really thought about how the movie would affect me. The important thing at that point was to get it filmed. And I was having too much of a blast to worry.

From all those days spent with Sean, my happiest memory is standing on the pitcher's mound, throwing him batting practice in the gloaming, just a couple of would-be professional baseball players whose lives went in other directions.

●

We were only a few days away from being finished with filming, and I was exhausted. The latest crisis occurred when a woman who had given us permission to film in her home suddenly became a nervous wreck when crew members began moving her furniture.

The next day, we began filming at noon. The goal was to get a few more baseball scenes in Norway, but it had rained and the field was a mess.

I ran into Jim Van Scoyoc, and we drove to Blairstown to get some ag lime to help dry out the Norway diamond. When we returned, we began walking toward the baseball field, I overheard one of the production assistants on the phone.

"You've got me kidding me," he said in a shocked tone.

"What's going on?" I asked.

"Our helicopter just went down."

I turned toward Jim, ashen-faced.

"I think Tony Wilson's on that helicopter."

22
Not in the Script

Jim and I walked to the north parking lot at Norway High School, where a crowd had gathered. Actors had emerged from their trailers to find out what was going on. Facts were elusive; I wasn't even entirely sure that Tony Wilson had been on the helicopter, but I had an ominous feeling that he had.

A day or so earlier, Tony had mentioned to me that it was one of his dreams to work behind the camera, that filmmaking was his true love. He had hoped he might be able to do so from the helicopter.

Then word arrived. There had been three people on the helicopter: Tony, the pilot and a cameraman. The camera operator, 50-year-old Roland Schlotzhauer from Lenexa, Kan., had been killed. Tony and the pilot had been injured, but nobody knew yet how seriously. They were conscious, and were being rushed to University of Iowa Hospitals in Iowa City.

I was shocked and heartbroken. I had met Roland earlier, while we were filming in the stressed-out woman's home in Cedar Rapids. And now he was dead, killed while filming our movie? This wasn't in the script. Our project was designed to bring joy and inspiration to people, not sadness.

In the parking lot, Sean Astin led the entire group, more than 100 people, in prayer. The tears rolled. I remembered thinking, "Why did this have to happen, Lord? So many miracles had occurred to bring this movie to life. Why this? Why now?"

I called Laurie; she was at the neighborhood swimming pool with Robin Evans, David's wife. Then I left for the hospital.

My cell phone rang constantly. I ignored it. I really didn't want to talk to anyone.

"Kent isn't one of those people who freak out," Laurie says. "He just gets really quiet. He kept saying, 'Laurie, we've got to pray,' and we would. That whole time he was saying, 'We've got to pray, Laurie. We've got to pray.'"

•

One of the first reports from the accident scene indicated that Tony might have broken a bone but otherwise appeared healthy. When we arrived at the hospital, I soon discovered that his injuries were quite a bit more serious. He was, in fact, fighting for his life.

There was a smashed vertebra in his back. Bone fragments had lodged in his spinal column and needed to be removed. All the ribs were broken on the right side of his chest; five were broken on the left side. He also suffered from a punctured lung.

The tibia bone in his left leg had popped out of the ankle. Doctors weren't sure they could save his leg.

Tony and I had become as close as brothers during the frantic years leading up to the movie. I knew he was a man of strong faith. He wanted nothing more than to make movies that families could enjoy. The man has a good heart, let me just put it that way.

"The Final Season" was his idea, and it never would have happened without him. His fingerprints were on everything, from the script to the budget. The fact that the movie was even being filmed was a testament to Tony Wilson's steadfast refusal to give up on the idea.

I knew he wouldn't give up now, and he didn't.

I remained at the hospital until 2 a.m. I don't think I've ever prayed so hard, for Tony, for the pilot, and for Roland's family.

But there also were practical concerns. We shut down filming on Friday, the day of the accident, but the plan was to resume on Saturday and finish on Sunday. If the movie was to be completed, we had no other choice. Contracts had been signed. Actors and crews had other jobs to go to next. Millions of dollars had been invested – some of those dollars by our friends and family members – in completing the movie on time.

It was up to us to fulfill Tony's dream.

●

On Sunday, the last day of filming, we worked from 10 a.m. until perhaps 2 a.m. Monday. It was an exhausting, emotionally draining day.

Tony's condition had stabilized, but he was far from out of the woods, and concern for his well-being hung over everything.

That afternoon, while we were filming inside a Cedar Rapids bank, Tony's wife, Roxanne, and daughter, Julia, showed up.

"Thanks for continuing," Roxanne told the cast and crew. "This is what Tony would want."

I'll never forget that. We all needed to hear it. It pushed us across the finish line.

Nor will I soon forget the atmosphere early the next morning, as we filmed in the parking lot. It was the scene in the movie in which the school bus driver suffers a heart attack. We pushed the bus back and forth to make it rock.

Then it began raining. About 1:30 a.m., David Mickey Evans announced, "It's a wrap."

Jim, Sean, David and I stood on top of the bus, tired and drenched by the rain, and drank a shot of Scotch together to celebrate the end of the final scene. Someone filmed it so Tony could enjoy it when he recovered.

Then we said a prayer for everyone.

●

I never did get an answer to my question, "Why did this have to happen, Lord?" My parents would have told me that it was a test of my faith, that I should trust that God acted in ways that we can't always understand at the time.

It wasn't fair, or right, to feel sorry for myself. Many people would have loved to be in my shoes, to have a movie filmed about one of the best moments of their life. And I was grateful beyond words that Tony and the pilot were still alive.

But it wasn't easy. I will always feel terrible about the camera operator who died. I can't speak for Jim, but a man died filming a movie about my life. To this day, I wish there were something I could do to change it, yet I know there isn't. All I can say is that it still weighs on me, and it's certainly something I will never forget or take lightly.

●

For Tony, the road back has been long and difficult. His leg was saved, but he had to learn to walk again. At first, he could stand up only by balancing himself on parallel bars. He advanced to a walker, and then to crutches. To this day, he favors his left leg occasionally, but he walks on his own.

But the same determination that got the movie written and filmed served Tony well during his rehabilitation.

He said he was inspired by a photograph that showed him pitching batting practice to Sean Astin. He said he wanted to be able to throw batting practice again someday.

When a reporter asked David Mickey Evans about Tony, he said, "He's the guy who saw it all the way through. It was literally a work of blood, sweat, tears and love."

Years ago, Reader's Digest used to publish a feature called "The Most Unforgettable Character I've Met." My choice would have to be Tony Wilson.

It's an honor to call him my friend.

23
Hollywood

Just because you've made a movie doesn't mean anyone is going to see it.

For that, we needed to attract a distributor, a company that would book and deliver our movie to theaters across America and, we hoped, the world. We could always go straight to DVD, the fate of many films these days, but none of us wanted to do that.

After filming, I returned to my principal's job, and David Mickey Evans returned to his Hollywood studio, where he proceeded to edit, add music and perform the thousands of behind-the-scenes tasks required to bring "The Final Season" to life.

The filming had attracted the imagination of people in Cedar Rapids and much of Iowa, and there were enough stories done about the movie that I returned to work something of a local celebrity. That was good – people were enthusiastic about seeing the film – but it also caused some folks to assume that I had suddenly become wealthy. Hardly. Like the other investors, I was eagerly waiting the release of the movie so we could get paid back.

In the fall of 2007, David told us he was ready to show us what amounted to a rough draft of the movie, and we made arrangements to meet him in Des Moines. But for some reason, a secretary had assigned the name "Steve Evans" to his airplane tickets (one of our producers is named Steve), and when David disembarked the plane during a layover in Denver, airline officials would not let him get back on. So he returned to Hollywood.

I couldn't stand it. If the movie was finished, or almost finished, I wanted to see it. Finally, I called David and asked him if Jim Van Scoyoc and I and our wives could see a screening if we went to Los Angeles.

Sure, David said. That would be wonderful.

Hollywood, here we come.

●

We left Cedar Rapids about 6 a.m. on the Sunday before Thanksgiving and arrived in Los Angeles sometime that afternoon.

As we were headed to the baggage claim area, Sean Astin called. I had told him we would be arriving, and he said he might be able to meet with us.

"Aren't you out here?" he asked. "You said you were going to call."

Just got in, I replied. I'll call you back when we get settled.

No sooner had I hung up and started down the escalator to the baggage area than I spotted Sean Astin standing at the bottom, with David Mickey Evans right next to him, giant grins on their faces. They didn't have to do this; it's the type of people they are.

"We'll give you an hour to get settled at the hotel," David said. "Then we'll be back to pick you up and take you to the screening."

When we arrived, Sean and Christine Astin were there, as well as Powers Boothe. David had wine, beer, soda pop and snacks available. I was pinching myself. It felt very weird to be there.

The lights dimmed, and the movie began.

It was the fastest two hours of my life.

On the flight to Los Angeles, Jim and I discussed how we would react if we didn't like the movie. We trusted David, but you never know how somebody is going to portray your life on screen. We agreed that we would be gracious and complimentary, no matter what, because we knew how much of his life he had invested in this project.

Well, our acting skills were not required. We both loved it. The story was compelling, Iowa and Norway looked gorgeous, the humor was sharp and the characters were easy to identify with. I couldn't have been happier. I felt we had done the Norway story proud.

Toward the end, when Powers Booth, portraying Jim, points to Sean Astin, portraying me, and Sean points back, I just about lost it. There were tears rolling down my face. Laurie was squeezing my hand, because I was trembling.

In the final scene, when Sean places the game ball in the Norway trophy case, I couldn't take it any longer. "I've got to get out of here," I told Laurie, and stood to leave. I didn't want the movie folks to see me bawling like some teenage girl watching the death scene in "Titanic."

The instant I stood up, the lights came on, and the first person I ran into was David Mickey Evans. We embraced in a big bear hug.

"Thank you, thank you, thank you," I said.

●

The new year arrived, and we still did not have a distributor. Tony Wilson was scrambling to find someone at the same time he was recovering from the helicopter accident.

We soon received some great news. "The Final Season" had been chosen to be shown at the Tribeca Film Festival in New York City. We were one of a dozen sports-related films that would be shown during the portion of the festival sponsored by ESPN.

Perfect. Our world premiere would be held at the end of April in New York City. I had been there once before, on a high school trip to the United Nations.

Our hope was that the film would generate enough buzz, or word of mouth, to convince a distributor that we were theater-worthy. This was our best, and perhaps final, shot.

Expectations were sky-high in the Cedar Rapids area. People started dreaming that the Norway baseball field might join the Dyersville ballpark where "Field of Dreams" was filmed as a tourist attraction. A contingent of 50 people from Cedar Rapids decided to attend the premiere. Laurie and I decided to take our two girls and our parents.

Once there, we were joined by David, Sean, Powers, Tom Arnold and Rachael Leigh Cook. This was becoming a very big deal.

On the night of the premiere, we had so many family members there that Laurie and I had to split up to travel to the theater. So there I sat, in the back of a taxi, in the middle of New York City, on the way to the world premiere of a movie about my life, with Kendrie on one side of me and Kylee on the other.

Tears streamed down my face.

"What's the matter, Daddy?" Kendrie asked me. "Are you sad?"

I squeezed her arm.

"No, honey, these are tears of joy."

•

The initial reaction was positive.

Jeffrey Lyons of NBC's "Reel View" called our movie "a wonderful story about baseball, tradition, learning lessons in life and the refusal to give up. 'The Final Season' will inspire and entertain everyone."

And Sports Illustrated awarded the film three out of four stars.

But we still had no distributor. Each day that passed made it more unlikely that we would make it to theaters in 2007. Nobody involved with the movie wanted to wait another year. The window was closing.

It reminded me of standing in the third-base coach's box during the state championship game.

Two outs.

Two strikes.

Nobody on base, down by a run, game on the line.

Our movie needed another miracle.

24
Almost Famous

There were so many times when our movie was on the brink of not being made, it only seemed right that finding a distributor would occur at the last possible moment.

But, once again, when all seemed hopeless, we reached an agreement with Sony, which placed us with the Yari Film Group. "The Final Season" would hold its Iowa premiere on Oct. 7, 2007, a Sunday, then open on 1,100 screens throughout the country the following Friday.

I couldn't have been more excited, for many reasons. First, I was thrilled for Tony Wilson, who had poured much of his life into this. Second, I was happy for the people of Norway and the players on my team, who would get some much-deserved recognition. And, third, there was the practical matter of being able to finally repay all those friends, family members and fellow Iowans who had invested in the movie.

I was so excited, in fact, that I probably downplayed or dismissed some cautionary signs.

We would be opening in the fall, at the end of baseball season, when the thoughts of most sports fans already had turned to football. The ideal time for us would have been the opening of the season, when baseball has the sports stage to itself, but we didn't think we could wait another six months.

The other thing I learned during the moviemaking process is that it takes money to make money, and we didn't have much left. Our advertising budget was significantly less than what was required for a national movie.

My hope was that enough people would enjoy the movie the opening weekend that the word of mouth would generate free publicity – and more moviegoers – for us.

If they saw it, they'd love it. Of that I was certain.

•

We held the Iowa premiere at the Galaxy Theater in Cedar Rapids. Chet Culver, Iowa's governor, arrived with his wife, Mari. Tom Arnold and Powers Boothe came, too. We even set up a little red carpet line that they could walk along, fielding questions from reporters.

"A home run," Culver said when the movie ended.

The reaction was great, but I have to admit, the audience was stacked in our favor. Many of the players from my Norway team attended the premiere, and I joined them at dinner afterward, where they signed movie posters and other items.

The next week, the players and I were invited to attend the movie at a reception in Vinton. I bought the first two rounds of drinks, to make up for the steak dinner they didn't get after they won the semifinal game during the state tournament. They got a kick out of that.

Being with those boys – now grown men with their own families – was as rewarding an experience as I've ever had. Teachers and coaches don't often get to see their classes or teams years later, to see how they've turned out. The Norway players turned out exactly as I would have expected. They weren't just champion baseball players, they were champion human beings.

I didn't know how much my life might change because of this movie. As I indicated earlier, I had become fairly well known in the Cedar Rapids area, but I didn't know what else to expect. Would Jay Leno come calling? Conan? Doubtful, but you never know.

I had begun accepting some speaking engagements in the area. It started as a way to tell people about the movie, but I also found it rewarding to try to inspire groups, especially young people, with our story. Never give up, I'd tell them. Look at what happened to us.

The night before we opened nationwide, I couldn't sleep.

What do you have planned for me next, God?

•

How about a big heaping dose of reality?

Looking back, we didn't really have a chance; we were just too inexperienced to realize it.

The movie opened well in Iowa, not just because the story is set there, but also because people had heard about it and looked forward to seeing it. That wasn't the case in the rest of the country, because we didn't have enough advertising money to let them know we were coming.

And that opening weekend is everything. It's when movies bring in most of their money. And a big opening weekend means theater owners are more inclined to keep you around, giving you the time necessary to generate positive word of mouth.

The professional critics didn't help, either. Our story was too sentimental and corny – they loved using that word, of course – for them. We knew that was a possibility, but there are plenty of examples in which moviegoers overrule the verdict of critics, if they are given enough time to discover the movie on their own.

We didn't have the time. The number of theaters we played in dropped from 1,100 that opening weekend to 330 the next.

It soon became clear that we weren't going to bring in enough money to cover our costs. Writing that sentence still makes me sick to my stomach. Laurie and I lost money, too, but I'll always feel guilty that people I know and love believed in our movie and lost money on it.

Here's the thing: I still think I was right. To this day, I hear from people who have seen "The Final Season" on cable and tell me how much they enjoyed it. "When did this come out?" they'll ask. "I don't remember hearing anything about it."

It's that kind of reaction that makes me think our movie still has one final miracle left, that it will tap into an audience and become the sort of baseball movie that is shown every year, like "Field of Dreams," the kind of movie that baseball fans will want to add to their DVD collections.

It's just a dream, but this was a movie that dreams made possible. It deserved a better ending.

●

Those were difficult weeks. I went from daydreaming about talk-show appearances to thinking about how we were going to tell people they weren't getting their money back.

School kept me busy, but I felt a little restless. Working on the movie had opened my eyes to other opportunities, and I was interested.

One of the friends I made during the project was Steve Brady, the president and chief executive officer of Community Savings Bank in Edgewood, who was our banker for the movie.

I saw a lot of Steve, and we liked each other. His wife, Donna, and Laurie hit it off as well. They went with us to New York City to the Tribeca

Film Festival, and to Los Angeles for a screening with the cast and crew members.

In the fall of 2007, Steve asked whether I would do a baseball-themed commercial for the bank, and I agreed. The next spring, he said bank officials were attending a business expo in Cedar Rapids, and he wanted to know whether I could spend some time in their booth. Sure.

That night, at dinner, I told Steve I was at a point in my life at which I needed a new challenge. "I've been in education 23 years, 16 as a principal," I said. "I'm good at what I do, but I'm spending way too much time with other people's kids and not my own. If you ever have anything open in your bank, let me know.

"I know it's tough to hire friends. I guarantee you one thing: I'll know if it's successful or not. You'd never have to fire me. I'd quit before that happens."

Steve was intrigued, and said he would think about it.

I heard back the next day, and my life was about to change directions again.

25
Heading for Home

————————————

Steve Brady sent me an e-mail the next day, saying he had talked with his senior leadership team and they were enthusiastic about my joining the bank.

I met with them in April. They were creating a new job, called relationship manager. The person would be responsible for building relationships with current customers and clients, to see what their needs were and whether the bank could do anything else for them. In addition, he or she would, it was hoped, attract new business for the bank.

"This is exactly what I want to do," I told them.

My principal's job and my work on the movie had introduced me to a broad array of people in the Cedar Rapids area. I've always prided myself on my ability to get along with people, and I thought I could do a good job of representing the bank's interests.

I love forming new relationships. I've done it my entire life.

They grilled me for two hours.

Why are you willing to leave your education career? Are you going to regret leaving it a few months later? Are you sure this is what you want to do?

Great questions.

•

Filming the movie was like getting a crash course in all the different opportunities that life presented. I loved being the Oak Ridge principal, but I had done it for five years, and it felt as if my career there had peaked. It was similar to the feeling I had when I pursued the building head position in Belle Plaine after several years of teaching.

As I've explained, being a school principal is like being on call 24 hours a day. I worried about every student, every teacher and every staff member every single day. After the movie, my heart just wasn't in it as much, and that wasn't fair to anybody.

There were three other reasons – the only reasons, really – that I needed to consider a change: Laurie, Kendrie and Kylee.

Laurie is the CEO of the Stock household, and she's great at it. She left her teaching job to stay with the girls and has never regretted it. She's involved in all aspects of our girls' lives, from school to church, and her piano-playing talent has made her a popular accompanist at school musicals and weddings and for the church band.

But Laurie needed some help. Well, to be fair, she was doing fine without my help, but I wanted to be there more than I was. Between being a principal and being preoccupied with getting a movie made, my family was getting squeezed out, and I wanted to change that.

I wonder whether it was the same feeling my father had when he decided to get his teaching degree and leave the Firestone factory. He had put his children first. I felt compelled to do the same.

The bottom line: I was spending more time helping other people raise their children and not enough time raising my own two daughters. They were still young enough that I felt I could get back some of the time with them I had missed.

The bank officials must have accepted my explanation, because they offered me the job, and I accepted.

●

I immediately knew I had made the right decision. The new job is exciting and a wonderful challenge.

When he left farming, my Grandpa Lee started working at a bank in McCallsburg. He always seemed to enjoy the work – certainly more than he enjoyed farming – and I wonder whether, subconsciously, that factored in my decision to seek the bank job.

There was another family tie: My dad had worked as a bank teller in his summers off from school.

I don't want to leave the impression that the decision to leave Oak Ridge was easy. Far from it. I had led the team that got that school up and running, and I'll always be proud of that legacy.

But I wanted to watch my daughters grow up.

●

Kendrie is 10 years old now. She's a very quiet, shy and reserved young lady. She's the sort of child who follows the rules and becomes frustrated when others don't. If Laurie doesn't follow a recipe to the letter – say, adding a teaspoon and a half of sugar instead of a teaspoon – Kendrie will point it out to her, she says.

Kendrie loves music, loves to dance and loves sitting in her grandparents' laps. It has been fun watching her grow up.

Kylee, 9, is much more aggressive. She's like me. She likes the spotlight. Laurie tells a story of how Kylee went after a little bully one day, and the boy said, "Kendrie's brother is mean." (Kylee had short hair then.)

She has a free spirit, but she's also the first one to offer you a hug. She can drive Kendrie crazy by telling her, in public, "I love you, Kendrie."

When we were filming the movie, somebody mentioned that I must have been disappointed that I didn't have two boys to play baseball with.

"My love is baseball," I responded, "but my daughters love dance and piano. It's my hope that they follow their love, and it takes them to great places much like baseball has done for me."

I've taught them about the St. Louis Cardinals and Bob Gibson; they've taught me about Hannah Montana.

It's a good deal.

●

I've got another girl, of course.

Laurie and I have been married 11 years now, and her talent and patience continue to amaze me. During filming of the movie, she'd bring the girls to the set each day, making sure they were part of a once-in-a-lifetime event, but also making sure that they saw their father.

Both of us think that God led us together, and nothing has happened in these 11 years to persuade me otherwise. When we first got married, I think my religious background brought her closer to God. After the trials of the movie and the principal's job, she was the one who brought me closer.

I've been on and coached some great teams in my life. This one is the best. No contest.

Epilogue

I'd like to share two final memories with you.

In October 2006, I received a call from Terry Trimpe, one of the producers of the movie. Terry had grown up in Lisbon and had actually played baseball for Jim Van Scoyoc at Amana High School – coaching there was Jim's first job out of college. A chance meeting between them led to Terry's involvement in our movie. He was invaluable when it came to fundraising.

Terry said he had two extra tickets to the fourth game of the World Series between the St. Louis Cardinals and the Detroit Tigers. Did I want them?

Absolutely. And I knew whom I was going to take – my dad, who had taken me to so many games in St. Louis when I was a boy.

Dad, typically, asked how much the tickets cost. Nothing, I replied. It's a gift.

Terry and his friend, Ron Armstrong, joined Dad and me on the 5½-hour trip south. As soon as we entered Missouri, it began to rain, and it was pouring when we reached the stadium. The public address announcer said the game was being delayed, so we sat in the rain for about three hours until the game was finally postponed.

This was a Wednesday night. The announcer said all Game 4 tickets would be honored two nights later, on Friday night. In other words, the Game 4 tickets were now Game 5 tickets.

I arrived back in Cedar Rapids at 3 a.m. I had to be at work four hours later, but I didn't care. If the Cardinals won Thursday night, we would have a chance of seeing them clinch their 10th World Series. That night, my dad and I (he stayed at our house) watched the Cardinals win Game 4 on television, high-fiving each other like a couple of grade school kids.

The four of us returned to St. Louis the next night, Oct. 27, 2006, and it was as magical as I had hoped it would be. The Cardinals won, 4-2, and as David Eckstein was accepting his most-valuable-player trophy, I was hugging my personal MVP and hero in Section 268. We might have set a record for the longest bear hug.

It probably took two hours to drive five blocks to get back on the interstate, but we didn't mind being part of the spontaneous parade. My cell phone was ringing constantly with friends congratulating me, including one from David Mickey Evans, who knew how important the Cardinals were to me.

I told you how, when I was a boy, Dad woke us up to go see Bob Gibson pitch, creating a lifetime memory for the family. I'd like to think I returned the favor, but it will be a long time before I can ever repay all he's done for me.

•

"OK, girls, get aggressive."

I was coaching volleyball again. There were 11 players on my team, including two who had become quite special to me – my daughters, Kendrie and Kylee.

This was a beginners' volleyball league for girls age 8 to 10. Our team name was "Little Pride" and we practiced at Oak Ridge Middle School.

This was as much fun as any coaching job I had ever had. The girls were enthusiastic and the parents were supportive.

I had looked forward to coaching my girls, but I found that they reacted differently to me than the other girls did. Finally, I had to sit them down and explain the difference between encouragement and being mad. When I shout, "Let's go, girls!" in a loud tone of voice, that doesn't mean they have done anything wrong. It took my daughters a little while to get used to that, but they seemed to understand.

We played in two tournaments, and all the feelings came rushing back to me. It felt as if I were in Marshalltown with the Norway baseball team, or in Cedar Rapids with my Belle Plaine volleyball team. It reminded me how much I love coaching. I don't think my coaching career is over just yet.

●

"How do you want to be remembered?"

It's a great question, in real life as well as in a Hollywood movie, and it's one that I've reflected on quite often since my moviemaking adventure ended.

I love the bank job, and could see staying there a long time. I'm also still interested in young people, and coaching retains its appeal. For one thing, it keeps me involved in sports. Although I no longer work in schools, I'm still passionate about issues involving education, and I've wondered whether there's some way to make another contribution there.

Over the past few years, I have done more than 50 speaking engagements, trying to inspire business, civic and youth groups with the story of the baseball team that never gave up, not even when there were two outs, two strikes and nobody on. I truly enjoy it and hope to do more in the future. I can't imagine ever getting weary of talking about that unforgettable final season.

But I haven't answered the question yet: How do I want to be remembered?

Here's what I know: My goal is no longer to be a professional baseball player. Or to be known as a great baseball and volleyball coach. Or to be a movie star or producer. All those quests have occupied my time over the years, and while I wouldn't trade any of those experiences, they aren't what really matters.

What I've learned is that home matters a lot more than home plate, that family trumps careers, that the people you love are a lot more important than what you achieve.

I'd like to be remembered the way my dad is known – as a loving husband, father, friend and a man of faith. The game's not over and, God willing, I'm going to give it my best shot.

Acknowledgments

Kent Stock

In the past few years, as I have spoken around the state about Norway and the making of "The Final Season," so many people told me, "You should write a book," that I decided to believe them. As you will soon read in these pages, my family has been supportive in all my various endeavors, and this was no exception.

I'd like to thank my mom, dad, sister and brother for letting me commit our stories to print. I'd like to thank Tony Wilson for his friendship, inspiration, and support.

Here's another thank you to the many friends, former teammates and students who expressed encouragement about the book. I'd like to thank Victoria Fink and Francis Frangipane at Arrow Publications for their interest. Many thanks to Chad Kreel for his layout work. I'd also like to thank Ken Fuson for his tireless work.

Most of all, I'd like to thank my wife, Laurie, who has been a rock of support, patience, and encouragement. And what can I say about my beautiful daughters, Kendrie and Kylee, other than they are a daily source of love and inspiration. It would require a book much larger than this one to fully express what they mean to me.

Ken Fuson

First, I'd like to thank Kent and Laurie Stock for believing I could do this and for their extraordinary patience and good humor as I pried into their lives and missed deadlines. My buddies Jeff McMenamin, John Carlson, Mark Siebert, Tom Beaumont, Randy Evans and the Boyles brothers offered great support, as always.

Jay Wagner taught me unforgettable lessons about dealing with life's bad breaks with grace, dignity, humor and courage.

I'd also like to thank my parents and family for their unwavering support, even when they weren't sure that leaving my job to write a book in the middle of a terrible economy was such a wise choice; Sandra Martin, the wonderful teacher who first encouraged me to write and hasn't stopped since; Russ and Dixie Boyles, who gave me my first newspaper job and became lifelong friends; and Janna Booher and the members of the First United Methodist Church choir in Indianola, who offer friendship, love, hope, and beautiful voices on a weekly basis. Finally, thanks to Amy, Jared, Jesse and Max, for... well, for everything.